For

Tom and Dear
Daly

with best wishes,

Tom Kelaher

PUBLIC CATHOLICISM

EDITED BY THOMAS PATRICK MELADY

PUBLIC CATHOLICISM

THE CHALLENGE OF LIVING THE FAITH IN A SECULAR AMERICAN CULTURE

THOMAS P. MELADY • MARY CUNNINGHAM AGEE • REVEREND RICHARD JOHN NEUHAUS
WILLIAM J. BENNETT • HENRY J. HYDE • RALPH REED, JR. • MARY ELLEN BORK
DOUGLAS W. KMIEC • MICHAEL NOVAK • JOHN M. HAAS • LINDA CHAVEZ
DEAL W. HUDSON • CHRISTOPHER H. SMITH • JOHN ENGLER • MICHAEL A. FERGUSON

Our Sunday Visitor Publishing Division
Our Sunday Visitor, Inc.
Huntington, IN 46750

To my first grandson,
Nicolas Melady Morin

Previous Books by Thomas Patrick Melady

Profiles of African Leaders
White Man's Future in Africa
Faces of Africa
Kenneth Kaunda of Africa
Revolution of Color
Western Policy and the Third World
House Divided (co-author)
Development Lessons for the Future (co-author)
Burundi: The Tragic Years
Uganda: The Asian Exiles
Idi Amin: Hitler in Africa (co-author)
The Ambassador's Story
Catholics in the Public Square (editor)

TABLE OF CONTENTS

Introduction

Public Catholicism versus private Catholicism is the center of the current debate. Should practicing Catholics express their opinions influenced by faith in the public square? Should they, influenced by faith, campaign for legislation and regulations that reflect Catholic teaching? Or should Catholics quietly practice their faith and regard it as a private matter, not related to the position they may take on public matters?

On November 17-18, 1995, 750 people participated in the Washington, D.C., Conference on issues in public affairs of interest to Catholics. The resounding theme of the Conference was that Catholic lay people should use all effective means in a democracy to influence public policy. They should in effect practice public Catholicism, and consequently, both in their personal lives and in their roles as citizens, they should campaign for the implementation of their faith-inspired teachings into the traditions and laws of their community, state, and nation.

The laws in Western democracies should represent the will of the people. Therefore Catholics living in these democractic societies have an obligation to use their influence so that the laws of the country reflect Catholic teachings.

Catholics living in the United States accept the covenant of the Constitution. They are not there to impose but to express their opinions and to play a role in obtaining the "best deal" possible for the teachings of the Church.

This can only be done by persuasion. It should only be done in a civil manner, recognizing that citizens of different faith traditions do not always accept Catholic teachings on some beliefs that are central to the practice of the Catholic faith.

But Catholics, enjoying like all citizens the rights of free expression in a democracy, should be as effective as they can in obtaining the "best deal" possible for the Church. And their way of doing this should reflect the traditions and practices of a democracy. Their method should be courteous, and all forms of extreme rhetoric should be avoided.

In Chapter I, "From a Lonely Minority to a Strong Presence," I review the history of the Catholic presence in the United States. From their early roots in Maryland, where in the pre-Revolutionary period English-speaking Catholics were allowed to practice their religion, up to 1776, they numbered slightly more than one percent of the population.

As their numbers grew from immigration to the United States from Europe in the nineteenth century, suspicions about Catholics turned into bigotry. Catholics remained a lonely minority throughout all of the nineteenth century, but they loved the freedom and the economic security that the country gave them. Whatever political, religious, or economic problems that Catholic Americans might have had in the nineteenth century, they were minor in comparison to the problems that they left behind in the "old country."

The twentieth century saw a Catholic candidate for President, Al Smith, defeated. Many voted against him because he was Catholic. A little more than three decades later, the second Catholic, John F. Kennedy, was elected.

Catholics at the end of the twentieth century constitute slightly more than 25 percent of the population in the United States. They have been and remain loyal Americans. They also have been, for the most part, faithful Catholics.

Michael A. Ferguson, Executive Director of the Catholic Campaign for America, in Chapter II, "Public Catholicism in the Twenty-First Century," points out that public Catholicism "begins with a spiritual recommitment to the Lord." This, he points out, is done in a uniquely Catholic way and is followed by translating that spirit into action by transforming and healing our culture and our nation.

In Chapter III, "American Democracy: Compatibility With the

Faith," Professor Douglas W. Kmiec brilliantly analyzes how an American democracy by its nature is compatible with the Catholic faith. He alerts us, however, to the danger in contemporary life of those who would seduce this compatibility.

Father Richard John Neuhaus in Chapter IV, "Can Catholic Americans Be Trusted in the Public Square?" responds to that question by issuing a clear call for active participation by Catholics in the public square and calling all Americans to consider their understanding of religion and public affairs. He challenges us, "Be not afraid to engage the truth. . . ."

Mary Cunningham Agee in Chapter V, "A Call to Holiness," illustrates how those in everyday life can respond to the call to holiness. This, as the author points out, is the basis for a life that is also committed to public Catholicism.

In Chapter VI, Mary Ellen Bork, writer and social commentator, recognizes a special calling for Catholic women. "The Role of Catholic Women in Building a Culture of Life" is based on the premise that Catholic women have a vital part to play in defending a culture based on truth, including the intrinsic value of motherhood, and the complimentarity of the relationship of women and men.

The importance of personal commitment is also emphasized by Deal Hudson, Editor of *Crisis* magazine, in Chapter VII, "What Cradle Catholics Take for Granted." Dr. Hudson traces the journey of a Baptist minister to the Catholic Church. He illustrates the critical importance of taking the gift of faith seriously.

The remaining chapters in this book are more directly related to the contemporary challenges facing people living in a country like the United States.

Dr. William Bennett, former Secretary of Education, in Chapter VIII, "A Catholic Perspective to the Cultural War," lays out a clear plan for Catholics in the United States to gain their objectives through redirection of the culture.

Michael Novak, the 1994 Templeton Prize Winner and Director of Social and Political Studies at American Enterprise

Institute, in Chapter IX, recalls the impact of Vatican Council II and the subsequent sweep of freedom in Eastern Europe.

Dr. Ralph Reed, the Executive Director of the Christian Coalition, in Chapter X documents the emerging partnership of Catholics and Evangelical Protestants in restoring historic Christian values to the public square.

Congressman Henry Hyde, Chairman of the Judiciary Committee of the U.S. Congress and a long-time crusader for human rights, in Chapter XI, and Congressman Christopher Smith, in Chapter XII, both call upon Catholic citizens to assist them in their desire to apply Catholic teachings to the challenges they face in the U.S. Congress.

Michigan Governor John Engler spoke at the banquet of the Catholic Campaign for America's first national Conference. In Chapter XIII, "Be Not Afraid: Look the Adversary in the Eye," Governor Engler calls for courage in the public square and illustrates the reforms he has accomplished in Michigan.

In the remaining chapters, syndicated columnist Linda Chavez and moral theologian Dr. John Haas conclude with very cogent observations. Ms. Chavez in Chapter XIV points out that Catholics with core beliefs can still have different approaches to applying Catholic teachings. Her "Issues and Diversity: A Catholic Perspective" is followed by Dr. John Haas with "Catholic Identity: Getting the Message Out," in Chapter XV, a reflection that will leave every reader feeling very proud to be a Catholic.

This collection of fifteen essays represents a comprehensive statement by a group of Catholic Americans deeply involved in the public square.

Thomas Patrick Melady
Editor

From a Lonely Minority
to a Strong Presence

American Catholics have so much to be thankful for. Our community has especially benefited from the greatness of our country, the guarantees of freedom, and the vitality of the American economy. Now as our country prepares to enter a new century and the third millennium of Christianity, let us look at where we American Catholics are situated in the spectrum of American life and politics. We know that our country is facing new and serious challenges to its moral greatness. How can we respond so we can assist the country that has done so much for us?

What Are American Catholics Doing?

How have we grown since the first years of the Republic? From the less than 30,000 Catholic lay persons constituting a little more than one percent of the population, Catholics now number over fifty-seven million, and slightly more than twenty-five percent of the total population. The American Catholic community operates the largest school system after the public school system. More than two million boys and girls are in the 7,210 Catholic elementary schools. In 1995 the Catholic secondary school system accounted for 652,054 students in the 1,350 Catholic high schools. And there were more than 650,000 students in the 235 Catholic colleges and universities.

Catholic support of a vast education system is matched by the care given to the sick and the needy. In 1995, the 605 Catholic hospitals cared for over fifty million patients. There are also 327 health care centers which assisted over two million people.

The mosaic of a caring community, inspired by the historic Church teachings on social justice, also provided assistance to the homeless, the orphans, the victims of substance abuse, convicts and other people marginalized in our society. These programs designed to meet social needs are being carried out in every one of our thirty-six Archdioceses and 163 Dioceses in the United States by 1,926 special centers. Catholic Charities and allied groups provided services to over sixteen million Americans. The Society of St. Vincent de Paul, for example, distributed goods among the poor in 1990 and 1991 valued in excess of $160 million. Catholic Charity agencies in 1993 served over 10.6 million people in need.

Inner Cities

The broad sweep of services to people by the U.S. Catholic community is breathtaking. Education receives heavy emphasis in the inner cities to serve the social needs of the lowest socioeconomic residents. In 1993, more than 900 Catholic elementary schools and 101 Catholic high schools were in the inner cities.

The services of the American Catholic Church exist to help not only Catholics but persons of all religious affiliations. These are moving examples of a Church in service to the people, as was Jesus Christ when He walked through the communities of the Holy Land. He cared for the sick. He showed concern for the marginalized. He was compassionate to the poor. He set the example for you and for me. And thousands of priests, nuns, lay missionaries, and lay volunteers are following the example of Jesus.

How the Catholic Community Has Grown

Catholic services to the people of the nation were not always so extensive. The Catholic community at the birth of the Republic in 1776 was not only a small fraction of the nearly four million population, but it had no real influence in the early days of the United States. The Catholic community in 1776 was a lonely minority. This condition was true not so much because the Catholic community constituted such a small percentage of the population but for other reasons. As followers of the ancient rights and beliefs of the Catholic Church, its adherents seemed odd and different to their neighbors, who were overwhelmingly Protestant.

The very few Catholics in what is now called New England were the objects of ridicule from their neighbors, who predominantly adhered to the simple rites and beliefs of the Congregational churches. In my home state of Connecticut, it was dangerous in the early days of the Republic for a priest to celebrate Mass. Catholics living in New York and Philadelphia were in similar positions with their neighbors, who were, for the most part, members of the Reform, Episcopal, or Quaker congregations.

The bulk of the Catholic community in the first years of the Republic was in Maryland. Father John Carroll operated out of Baltimore in 1784 because of Lord Calvert's establishment of Maryland as a colony where English and Irish Catholics could enjoy the freedom to practice their own religion. The tradition of religious freedom for Catholics in Maryland continued through the early days of the Republic. Recognizing this, Pope Pius VI in 1789 declared Baltimore as the first diocese of the United States, with John Carroll as the first Bishop.

Outside of Baltimore: Suspicions

There were in the first years of the United States only a few cases of blatant oppression. But in that period, the majority of Americans viewed Catholics as alien to the new democratic spirit of the young Republic. Many early residents of the original thirteen states felt that Catholics were generally ignorant of the emerging ideas of democratic institutions because of their allegiance to the Pope. Catholic cultural traditions were not understood by most Americans in the beginning years of the American Republic.

The pioneer American Catholics, however, loved their newfound freedom. They had left either political oppression or economic hardship. While they were a distinct, small, and not influential minority in the United States, they remained faithful to their Church and by their actions, showed that they were good and loyal Americans.

Catholics had fought in the Revolutionary War in numbers exceeding their percentage in the population, and they were enthusiastic about the new Republic. It was certainly superior to the oppression, economic hardship, and chaos they had suffered in Europe.

This characteristic of patriotic loyalty remains with Catholics today.

Nineteenth Century

The years from 1800 to 1900 were years of mixed experiences for Catholics in the United States. They, on the one hand, benefited from the spirit of religious freedom and tolerance, but they also suffered from the significant anti-Catholic movements that brought harm and hardship to some of their members.

The commitment of the early American Protestant leadership to religious freedom generally prevailed over the forces of bigotry. Catholic immigrants from Europe came to the open shores of the United States in increasing numbers in the nineteenth century. In both the nineteenth and twentieth centuries, Catholics in Europe were never discouraged, by the periodic anti-Catholic outbursts, from immigrating to the United States. One reason for this was the religious turmoil in Europe. Catholics in Ireland were persecuted by the British Protestant governing class. Catholics in France and Italy saw the destructive nature of anticlericalism. Catholics in various parts of Germany and the Netherlands had problems with religious freedom, depending on the local ruler. The Austrian-Hungarian Empire, while Catholic-friendly, was full of ethnic rivalries.

And throughout all of nineteenth-century Europe, there were extreme economic hardships for the peasant and laboring classes. Our Catholic ancestors who immigrated to the United States were overwhelmingly from the nineteenth-century "underclass." Whatever hardships that faced Catholics in America, they were almost insignificant in comparison to their life in the "old country."

Increased Immigration

Suspicions about the increasing number of Catholic immigrants grew in the nineteenth century. Various extreme anti-Catholic groups organized riots against Catholics. They were so bad in 1844 that Abraham Lincoln, speaking in Springfield, Illinois, said:

> The guarantee of the rights of conscience as found in our Constitution, is most sacred and inviolable, and one that belongs no less to the Catholic than to the Protestant.

How would this increasing number of Catholics affect American institutions? During the last two decades of the nineteenth century, many of those who feared the growing Catholic presence joined the American Protective Association (APA). Members of the APA took an oath that included these words:

> I hereby denounce Roman Catholicism. I hereby denounce the Pope.

But these anti-Catholic statements did not prevail because the core Protestant leadership of our country remained committed to religious freedom.

Catholic Church: Friend of Labor

The overwhelming number of Catholic immigrants were workers; consequently the culture of the Catholic community was friendly to the labor class. This also meant that the priests and

Bishops were the sons, for the most part, of working families. The same was also true for women who joined religious orders. They were generally the daughters of the working class. Thus began in the United States the tradition of the Catholic Church being a friend of labor.

The identification of the Church with labor and social justice issues gave the Church great strength with the "underclass" of the nineteenth century. The American "underclass" was heavily Catholic. The Catholic community benefited at the end of the nineteenth century from two strong leaders: Pope Leo XIII in Rome and Cardinal Gibbons in the United States.

Cardinal Gibbons became the second son of America to wear a Cardinal's hat. He said of his country at ceremonies in 1887:

> The civil government of the United States holds over us the aegis of its protection without interfering with us in the legitimate exercise of our sublime mission as ministers of the Gospel of Christ. Our country has liberty without license and authority without despotism.

He, like all American Church leaders after him, was a loyal American.

Presence: Not Influence

The Catholic Church in the United States in the twentieth century was ready for a more significant role in the worldwide Catholic community. The formal announcement on this occurred on June 29, 1908, when Pope Saint Pius X, in his apostolic constitution *Sapienti consilio*, ended the mission status of the Catholic Church in the United States. At this time the fourteen million Catholics constituted around nineteen percent of the U.S. population. The Church had become a formidable *presence* in the United States.

Despite their increase in numbers, Catholics in the first decades of the twentieth century were not significant factors in the U.S. power structure.

The halls of power in federal and state governments, in the private sectors of banking, and the steel, fuel, transportation, and other major industries were devoid of Catholics in key positions. The first Catholics to arrive on the political scene were local politicians in Boston and New York. This further complicated the American Protestant community's public perception of Catholics since "big city" politicians did not convey the refined, cool image of statesmen.

Hoover-Smith Elections of 1928

The increased population and the strength of Catholics in the Northeast combined to influence the Democratic party in 1928 to nominate a Catholic, New York Governor Al Smith, for President. The Republican candidate was Herbert Hoover.

It was in many ways a bitter election. There was bigoted opposition to Al Smith. These attacks, not only against the Catholic Church, but especially against its members, were denounced by Herbert Hoover in the course of the campaign.

Herbert Hoover was elected. Within a few months after the 1928 elections, troubled by the prejudice so evident in the election debates, Protestant and Jewish leaders invited Catholic leaders to join them in establishing a national educational organization to fight religious prejudice. The National Conference of Christians and Jews thus came into existence.

The top Protestant leadership rejected the religious prejudices against Catholics in the 1928 elections as they had done in the previous century.

Roosevelt Administration

The Franklin Roosevelt administration was the first one that admitted Catholics to the inner circles of power and influence. Roosevelt also appreciated the unique role of the Vatican in world affairs, and in 1939 he established quasi-diplomatic relations with the Pope. The special envoy arrangement was a prelude to formal diplomatic relations established by President Ronald Reagan in 1984.

From the Roosevelt administration to the end of the twentieth century, Catholics increased in numbers to twenty-five or twenty-six percent of the population. And now the Catholic community has more influence than it has ever had in the United States.

At the end of the twentieth century, the American Catholic community is a mosaic on the one hand of a rich heritage, commitment, and belief, and, on the other hand, of doubt, confusion, and indecision.

Where Are American Catholics Going?

Catholic teachings on morality, the family, and virtue were similar to the teachings of all Christians in the nineteenth century. We know that the teachings were not always carried out. These inconsistencies were, in many cases, tolerated, but never approved as "rights."

Now in this period of history, the Catholic community still embraces the same traditional teachings, but many in the country no longer support these teachings, and in fact actively oppose them. The Catholic community is now frequently under attack by some civic leaders for advocating these values.

Catholics, privately living their faith, present few problems to those opposed to Catholic teachings. But when Catholics exercise their constitutional rights and advocate their beliefs in the public square, they are called bigoted by some opponents.

The special challenge for American Catholics today is making their *private* Catholicism *public*.

In a democracy like the United States and in the democracies of the Western world, it is lay people who should advocate their moral beliefs and, when appropriate, seek their enactment into the laws of the country.

There should be no doubt as to the authoritative source of Catholic teaching. It is the Pope and the Bishops. In a democracy it is the Catholic lay people who should advocate and seek to influence public policy with Catholic values. Pope John Paul II, in his encyclical *Evangelium Vitae* calls on lay persons to actively advocate and support core Catholic teachings on life. In fact, Catholic lay people have an obligation to campaign for the incorporation of basic Catholic teachings within the legal, constitutional, and legislative rules, traditions, and laws of this country. Papal advice can now be simply translated for American Catholics. Lay people should be active in the electoral process at the local, state, and federal levels. Their goal should be to *influence public policy* to come as close as possible to Catholic teachings.

This challenge exists at every level. In local communities, for example, Catholic lay persons should be the advocates of the application of Catholic teachings on the decisions made by school boards, county councils, and the like.

It is very clear from papal teachings that, at the state and federal levels where laws are enacted, Catholic lay persons should be active in influencing the drafting of legislation and in obtaining support for laws that reflect Catholic teachings.

Style and Method

We are Americans living in a pluralistic society. We live under and embrace the Constitution which has so protected American Catholics in the past. Our methodology should be to advocate. We cannot impose.

Our style of advocating should be that of a convinced believer and one who respects the rights of other citizens in a democracy to have another point of view. Let us avoid shrill voices, and let us never be self-righteous.

In working with our fellow Catholics we should seek unity in supporting core values. Our approaches to obtain them may vary, but the selection of a few key values as priorities should unite most of us.

American Catholics have benefited so much from this great country. Political liberty and economic security have given our community strength and happiness.

Our country, as it approaches the next century, needs a stronger, moral compass. Now is the moment to return something of value to a country that has given so much to us.

All the traditions and laws of the United States converge to encourage all citizens to play an active role in the public square. Both as loyal Americans and faithful Catholics, we should give the time and energy to advocate our convictions with our fellow citizens of all persuasions.

And when we do this, we should quietly say a prayer of thanksgiving to the Father of us all — one of thanks for our country and for our faith.

Public Catholicism
in the Twenty-First Century

Archbishop Fulton Sheen once said, "We are more often tempted to do good than we are to do evil. And it is a temptation that we don't often enough give in to."

You and I both know that temptation. And we can think of times when we have resisted and times when we have given in. I want to share with you a time when I gave in, because it is an illustration of the concept that I want to communicate to you today.

The Essence of Public Catholicism

I used to teach high school in the Bronx, and, as you can imagine, more than a few challenges come with the job of educating fifteen-year-olds in the inner city. From lighting fires in the classroom to falling asleep because they were up all night busing tables, city kids have plenty to keep them from focusing on their schoolwork. I had one student in particular, Brian, who came from a tough neighborhood, and it showed. He was physically bigger than most of the other students, certainly bigger than me, and his size and athletic ability made him a star on the football team. He rarely spoke or participated in anything academic, and his curt manner led one to believe that he didn't care much about anything other than himself. He hardly seemed a natural candidate for a spiritual retreat When I asked my students who might be interested in going, he was not the first to raise his hand. But through some conversation and some coaxing, he did come on

23

retreat, and it turned out to be one of the most important and transforming experiences of his young life. He became more aware of the Lord's love for him and the importance of his own spiritual and moral development. I received a letter from him recently and I'd like to share some of it with you.

> I have graduated from high school and soon will be entering the United States Army. I really have turned my life around recently, and I always think back to that retreat with you and the other guys. I never thought much about God or spirituality in my life before that weekend, but as I grow older, I begin to recognize that there are not many things I can do in my life that will have meaning without the Lord and His guidance. Thank you for the opportunity to let Jesus become a part of my life.

This story about Brian captures the essence of public Catholicism. It is through a personal and spiritual recommitment to our faith that we can most fully recognize the healing and transforming power of our faith and our God. When I encouraged Brian to explore what his faith meant to him on a very individual level, he was able to translate that personal sanctification into action, by getting his life together and encouraging others to do the same. He gave in to the temptation to do good, and he is a shining example of what we call public Catholicism.

Developing the Concept of Public Catholicism

When I became the Executive Director of the Catholic Campaign for America in 1995, I was thrilled to be able to take a more active role in developing the concept of "public Catholicism." It is an honor and a challenge to be able to address how we as a Catholic community in this country can deal with the problems that we face as a people and as a nation. Public Catholicism is an important concept for us to be able to grasp, and it will prove to be vitally important as we come to the close of the second millennium and charge into the third.

Public Catholicism begins with a personal spiritual

recommitment to the Lord in a uniquely Catholic way, and then translating that illuminating spirit into action by transforming and healing our culture and our nation.

But while it is true that we are looking to the future, we must remember that a movement with vision must also have a firm understanding of its past. As we head into the twenty-first century, it is necessary to look back at how we arrived where we are today. The modern American Church has its roots in the spirit of the Second Vatican Council, when reformers hastened the evolution of our Church and made it more engaging and, to use the current term, more "user-friendly." One of the central players in the reforms of Vatican II was the Archbishop of Krakow. As we all know, he was someone who would go on to shape our Church for years and generations to come. The Holy Father's role in Vatican II was one of guidance, leadership, and vision, and it is these qualities, along with the grace of the Holy Spirit, which have enabled him to chart a course for renewal as we and our Church approach the third millennium.

In recent encyclicals and pastoral letters, the Holy Father has been gradually outlining his vision for the spiritual and moral future of our Church. From a discussion of the culture of life in *Evangelium Vitae*, to reflections and guidance on economic theory and practice in *Centesimus Annus*, John Paul II has been one of the most pastoral and visionary leaders of the twentieth century, and indeed, an appropriate person to lead us toward the year 2000. I would like to draw your attention to two recent reflections of the Holy Father in particular, though, as they have particular significance to the mission of the Catholic Campaign and the theme of this weekend's convention.

The first is the encyclical *Veritatis Splendor*, or the "The Splendor of Truth." In it, the Holy Father discusses the meaning of Christ's message and the impact that should have on our personal conduct and our lives. He goes into some detail about the role of individuals in various governance systems, and how those systems should always place the highest value on the intrinsic goodness and dignity of the individual. In Western democracies this is particularly important since they depend on people's participation. Without the action of principled and morally sound individuals, any participatory system of government ultimately fails, and the Holy Father was explicit in urging citizens of participatory democracies to make themselves, and their actions, a force of goodness, justice, and compassion. Without it, our civilization is doomed to disintegrate like so many others have throughout the centuries.

But before we can have a constructive discussion about public activism and participation, we must come to terms with what that activism will add to public discourse and to society. We must sanctify and heal ourselves as individuals before we will be able to heal our culture. Activism must be founded on principle to have any real meaning.

A New Evangelization

In *Tertio Millennio Adveniente*, or "The Coming of the Third Millennium," the Pope calls us to embark upon a "super-Advent" if you will, a time of preparation, recommitment, and re-energization. When the Holy Father talks about the time leading up to the millennium, it is in terms of preparing oneself for a new era of hope, reconciliation, and understanding. If we are not properly prepared for that era, it will slip past us, an opportunity wasted. John Paul II specifically calls for "evangelization, or rather the new evangelization" to include opening the mission of the Church to areas of broad participation by the laity.

In Newark, New Jersey, in December 1995, he said, "As we prepare to celebrate the 2,000th anniversary of Christ's birth, we must recognize the need for the new evangelization, a new and vital proclamation of the Gospel aimed at integrating your faith ever more fully into the fabric of your daily lives." He recalled the words of the Second Vatican Council when he said "the Church must make a supreme effort to teach the objective truths of the moral order, form consciences, call people to conversion, and make present the inexhaustible riches of God's mercy. . . ."

The re-evangelization to which the Holy Father refers is not a difficult image to picture: He likened it to a seed of faith which is sown in Baptism and which must ripen into a rich harvest through service to God and to others as we carry it out to the whole world, so that we can sow it in the fields and vineyards. He recalled Jesus' reminder that the harvest is bountiful but the workers are few. Each of us can answer that call to the harvest and to the new evangelization by recommitting ourselves to Christ's Church and by heeding the pastoral words of the Holy Father.

Why must this be done? For nothing short of a transformation of our culture and of the world.

What makes this an important part of the Church's life in these next few years? John Paul is very clear on this point: This spiritual and personal renewal will *"illuminate* the mystery of man and *assist* in finding the solutions to the outstanding problems of our time." This is a vitally important point. He is calling us to personal sanctification and to public Catholicism, living our faith and carrying it with us throughout the world.

I am not going to run down a litany of the problems we are facing in our country today. We can be thankful that there is a growing sensitivity to the moral and cultural needs of our nation. But from our families, to the media, to our government leaders, there are challenges which face us in all walks of life, and they are challenges which are at the core of the need for public Catholicism. This Catholicism begins with a conscious and public recommitment to our faith. That is what the Holy Father is calling for in the pastoral letter on the third millennium, that is what he spoke about in 1995 when he visited our country, and that is what will create the dynamic forces which will inspire and empower us to heal the wounds that have been inflicted on our society. One needs to look no further than the collapse of communism for an example of the transforming power of prayer and personal and spiritual strength.

Spiritual revitalization and re-evangelization is at the heart of dutiful and civic public activism. As the Catholic Campaign mission statement reminds us, the Second Vatican Council encouraged us as a laity to become engaged in the sanctification of men and women and to renew the temporal order. It is precisely these instructions which John Paul II recalled in the 1994 encyclical *Veritatis Splendor*.

The Practice of Virtue

At the heart of the message of *Veritatis Splendor* and the call to public Catholicism is the practice of virtue. All things must be done within the practice of the virtue of temperance, to moderate our attachments to this world; the virtue of justice, to preserve our neighbor's rights; and in solidarity, following the Golden Rule and in keeping with the generosity of the Lord.

The most difficult, and consequently the most rewarding part of public Catholicism, then, is the convergence of the two virtues the Holy Father and our Church have outlined in the examples I have mentioned. On the surface, it seems quite simple: We are to renew the meaning of the Gospel in our own lives, and then turn that renewal outward to put it into practice in all that we do. But we know how challenging it is to live the simple message of Christ when he says, "Love one another as I have loved you." Similarly, it is challenging in this day and age of temptation, moral relativism, and secular humanism, to answer the Holy Father's call. It was in Baltimore that John Paul II spoke as clearly as ever with regard to public Catholicism when he said that

> . . . faith is always demanding, because faith leads us beyond ourselves. It leads us directly to God. Faith also imparts a vision of life's purpose and stimulates us to action. The Gospel of Jesus Christ is not a private opinion, a remote spiritual ideal or a mere program for personal growth. The Gospel is the power to transform the world! The Gospel is no abstraction: It is the living person of Jesus Christ, the Word of God, the reflection of

the Father's glory, the incarnate Son who reveals the deepest meaning of our humanity and the noble destiny to which the whole human family is called.

He went on to say that

Christ has commanded us to let the light of the Gospel shine forth in our service to society. How can we profess our faith in God's word and then refuse to let it inspire and direct our thinking, our activity, our decisions and our responsibilities toward one another?

The Holy Father, with these words, captured the essence of public Catholicism. He hit on the fundamental meaning of what it means to be a Catholic American today. It means standing up for the disadvantaged and the weak, from the unborn to the poor, the sick, the immigrant. It means respect for the dignity of the human person and of the family unit. It means welcoming the positive and constructive contributions of religious people to the public debate, not excluding them because of their commitment to their faith and their values.

The U.S. Catholic Conference released a letter on Catholic participation ("USCC Statement on Political Responsibility," November 1995) in the political process which properly touched on some of these issues and the fact that there are those on both sides of the political debates who miss the message of the Gospel as it inspires us to become publicly active. We must develop a consistent ethic of public activism to embrace *all* parts of the teachings of Christ and the Holy Father, and not simply follow those parts of the message which are most convenient for us.

Perhaps the most obvious and important reason for the need for public Catholicism was spelled out in the great encyclical *Evangelium Vitae*, or "The Gospel of Life." Though it was not the focus of the document, the Pope made some very serious analyses of democratic systems of governance. With regard to civil law and moral law, he said that "fundamentally, democracy is a system, and as such it is a means and not an end." Its "moral value is not automatic, but depends upon conformity with the moral law to which it, like every other form of human behavior, must be subject: in other words, its morality depends on the morality of the ends it pursues and of the means which it employs." I find these particular insights so important to the meaning of activism in the public square, and indeed, to anyone involved with public Catholicism. As someone trained in political science, I find that too often today the ideal of representative democracy is idolized without regard for the ideal of the common good. As we continue to experience turbulence and national crises, we find ourselves asking how these things could happen in the strongest and best governed country in the world. The answer lies in the moral foundation of that governance, and if that moral ground is shifting, the most stable government in the world will not be able to grow strong on top of it.

The Pope continued his remarks on this topic by saying, "The value of democracy stands or falls with the values which it embodies and promotes." It is insights like that which have drawn so many to the Church and which have elevated Pope John Paul II to his current position as the only truly global leader of the current time, and which have made our Church one of the most active forces in the promotion of justice, peace, and compassion. It is these virtues that he urged us not to make a matter of private opinion, but a beacon of hope for those around us and for our nation. It is in this context that the Holy Father urged us to testify to our faith and to participate more fully in the public square; to limit and work to eliminate actions and laws that violate the culture of life, and to replace them with provisions that are supportive of life, the family, and economic and social justice for all people.

Practicing Public Catholicism

In this context, the Catholic Campaign for America strives to promote the values of public Catholicism and to make them more accepted and practiced. At our leadership conference in Baltimore in 1994, we released the "Principles of Public Catholicism," which included the call to be faithful to the Holy Father, to be knowledgeable about Church teachings, and to be proud of our Catholic heritage. These were an important step toward defining and crystallizing what it means to be a public Catholic. But how is that put into practice in our public activism? What do these virtues mean in the context of the current political and social climate?

Today, we seek to put the principles of public Catholicism into practice in a real and substantive way, and we do so by announcing the main themes of the Catholic Campaign. The Catholic Campaign for America means a campaign that:

— Challenges our political institutions, popular culture, and media to embrace Judeo-Christian values and to help infuse them into American public life.

— Encourages recognition of the dignity of women and supports the life-giving and life-affirming role of women in society, asking the Blessed Mother to be our inspiration and guide.

— Enables parents to send their children to the school of their choice.

— Encourages our democratic institutions to move power from government bureaucracies closer to people.

— Encourages citizens to fill legislatures and public institutions with individuals who respect and defend the family and the "culture of life," particularly by encouraging crisis pregnancy support and adoption while seeking an end to abortion.

These campaign themes will be the driving force behind the growth of the Catholic Campaign for America and will serve to guide us as we engage ever more thoughtfully and forcefully in the public square.

We are here to harken the call of public Catholicism, and so the next time you are faced with the temptation to do good, I pray that you will be inspired to submit to that temptation entirely and wholeheartedly.

American Democracy: Compatibility With the Faith

Some years ago, John Courtney Murray was asked whether Catholicism is compatible with American democracy. Murray bluntly responded that such a question "is invalid as well as impertinent; for the manner of its position inverts the order of values. It must," he wrote, "be turned round to read whether American democracy is compatible with Catholicism."[1]

Obviously, Murray's point was that to be properly stated the emphasis of the question must recognize faith in God, not democracy (which after all is little more than faith in ourselves), as superior. John Paul II reminds of this as well in *Evangelium Vitae*, remarking that "Democracy cannot be idolized to the point of making it a substitute for morality or a panacea for immorality.[2] Fundamentally, the Holy Father instructs, "Democracy is a 'system' and as such is a means and not an end. Its 'moral' value is not automatic, but depends on conformity to the moral law to which it, like every other form of human behavior, must be subject."[3]

The relevant question today, therefore, for an American Catholic, and indeed for people of every faith tradition, is: To what ends is the American democracy dedicated?

• Is our American democracy dedicated to:

the recognition of the sacredness of human life

or

life's destruction — through the sanctioning of abortion, the promotion of contraceptive use by adult and minor alike, and the lifting of prohibitions against assisted suicide and other forms of euthanasia?

32

• Is our American democracy dedicated to:

strengthening the American family

or

its destruction through tax policies that penalize
families with children and necessitate two-income
households, laws that facilitate divorce, or ideologically-
driven agendas that falsely equate cohabiting
relationships, whether homosexual or heterosexual,
with sacramental marriage?

• Is our American democracy dedicated to:

the recognition of the irrelevancy of race in private
or public decision-making and the acceptance that we
are all created in the image and likeness of God

or

the aggravation of racial division through racial set-
aside, quota, or the labeling of the absence of preference
as racial discrimination?

• Is our American democracy dedicated to:

permitting educational resources that are raised
from the public citizenry at large to be spent freely
within a religious school that shares the faith of the
family,

or

the perpetuation of a public school monopoly that
often fails to educate in matters of competence and far
too often advocates a moral system that is antagonistic
to faith?

• Is our American democracy dedicated to:

a preference for limited government and federalism
as a way of affirming the extent to which men and

> women define their lives through participation within
> local community

or

> more and more public decisions becoming the
> subject of centralized, federal legislation imposing
> invariable and inescapable mandates that often cannot
> be met or met only with difficulty, added cost, and
> bureaucracy?

In short, is our American democracy still dedicated to the
proposition that we hold certain truths to be self-evident? Truths
that unashamedly acknowledge the existence of a Creator God.
Truths that hold life, liberty, and the pursuit of happiness as
inalienable rights derived from that God, and not as indulgences,
extended (or withdrawn) as a matter of legislative grace from a
presumptuous sovereign. Truths that recognize that the fate of our
republic, and our individual lives within it, depend upon a
Supreme Being.

Without God, We Can Do Nothing

Benjamin Franklin at the constitutional convention in 1787
reminded his bickering colleagues, who were frustrated at the time
by an impasse in the constitutional drafting, that "the longer I live,
the more convincing proofs I see of this truth — that God governs
in the affairs of men. And," Franklin asked, "if a sparrow cannot
fall to the ground without his notice, is it probable that an empire
can rise without his aid?"[4] More aptly, perhaps, can a democratic
empire situated smugly between two vast oceans and possessing
abundant personal and material resources continue to survive
without God's aid?

In our hearts, where God has lovingly written the great law of
nature, I believe we, as Americans — and especially as Catholic
Americans — know the answer. Just as no good thing is impossible
with God, so too, nothing truly good is possible without Him.

We may know this in our hearts, but in our heads, actions, and laws, God has too often not been affirmed, but denied. For the last thirty or so years, a period of tremendous cultural decline and turmoil in America, the Constitution, which by design gives preference to the free exercise of religion as the first of our civil bill of rights, has by interpretation been rendered neutral toward religion and faith. The recitation of mottos such as "In God We Trust" and "One Nation Under God" are tolerated, rather than happily embraced. And even this unenthusiastic toleration of God is possible only because, in the words of one Supreme Court justice, these expressions "no longer have religious purpose or meaning. The reference to divinity in the revised pledge of allegiance, for example, may merely recognize the historical fact that our Nation was believed to have been founded [past tense] 'under God.' "[5]

Cases from the Court's recent terms signal some greater tolerance for private religious expression and the belief that religion ought not be a disability from participating in public programs or receiving some public resources under very hedged conditions.[6] But this grudging allowance for people who desire to act upon their faith in public places is far less than the Supreme Court's earlier recognition that "We are a religious people whose institutions presuppose a Supreme Being."[7] It is certainly far less than Franklin's simple, yet genuine reminder of faith to his fellow constitutional delegates — do not forget that no empire can rise without God's aid.

The disassociation of God from American democracy is the most fundamental and far-reaching source of incompatibility with our faith. And it potentially subverts the American idea in its entirety. As Murray wrote, "the American proposition rests on the more traditional conviction that there are truths; that they can be known; that they must be held; for, if they are not held, assented to, consented to, worked into the texture of institutions, there can be no hope of founding a true City, in which men may dwell in dignity, peace, unity, justice, well-being, freedom."[8] In this, Murray was merely echoing George Washington, who wrote in his farewell message, "Of all the dispositions and habits which lead to political prosperity, religion and morality are indispensable supports. In vain would the man claim the tribute of patriotism, who should labour to subvert these great pillars of human happiness. . . . A volume could not trace all their connexions with private and public felicity." Washington framed the issue starkly: "Let it simply be asked," he said, "where is the security for property, for reputation, for life, if the sense of religious obligation *desert* the oaths which are the instruments of investigation in courts of justice?"[9]

Where, indeed? Some posit that man's own self-interest can propel the democratic engine. But self-interest rather quickly descends into rank selfishness. Rather than inspiring us to work in church congregation and community for matters of common good, it leaves men and women alone, divided or detached from each other and their neighbors. The sought-after end of constitutional argument in a merely self-interested republic is nothing more than "the right to be left alone." Individual is set against individual, each competing for the wealth of the market or the power of the state to gain, not solidarity, but advantage. In this society of radical individualism, "'right' is not a term relating to a moral order deriving from the [created] essences of [people and] things; it is simply a symbol flourished to assure the free functioning of self-interest."[10]

But a free functioning self-interest in a democratic context is just as likely to pursue evil as good. It is just as likely to see the unborn child as unwanted burden, rather than as extraordinary gift. It is just as likely to see one's own life as disposable at will, rather than as intrinsically valuable.

In the words of John Paul II, "this is the risk of an alliance between democracy and ethical relativism. . . . "[11] And as the Holy Father cautions, "as history demonstrates, a democracy without values easily turns into open or thinly disguised totalitarianism."[12]

Is this to be our future? If it is, it will only be because we have modernly forfeited our history premised upon the knowable truth of the "laws of nature" to which our nation committed itself in the Declaration of Independence. It is well past time to remind ourselves, and our fellow citizens, that Thomas Jefferson anchored our Republic squarely upon "the laws of nature and nature's God," and in doing so, he was drawing upon Hebrew, Catholic, and Protestant tradition going back over 500 years. Contrary to latter-day revisionism, this is not an embrace of the Enlightenment and the substitution of man for God, but a full scale endorsement of the proposition that the laws of the new American nation depend upon two sources — that written by God in creation, itself, and that found in God's revelation. And these two sources are not divergent, since of course they shared at the time of the founding, and they share now, the common origin in God himself. That is why Jefferson does not refer to merely the law of nature (singular), but the laws of nature (plural) — both that which God has planted within us and that which is revealed directly to us by written word. As one of the most influential writers at the time of the founding, Sir William Blackstone, wrote: "the revealed law . . . is the law of nature expressly declared to be so by God himself; . . . Upon these two foundations, the law of nature and the law of revelation, depend all human laws."[13]

Self-Evident Truth

I cannot deliver a complete course upon the laws of nature to which our nation must remain committed if faith and democracy are to remain compatible. Detailed and orthodox courses of instruction must be left for such places as Notre Dame, Providence, Catholic, Steubenville, Dallas, the tiny giants of Thomas Aquinas and Christendom College, and the thousands of Catholic secondary and elementary schools. And if in these or other places of learning, what is taught is neither detailed nor orthodox nor even Catholic then it is up to us, the Catholic laity and parents of America, to demand a full accounting.

It is possible, however, to outline some essentials.

First, we are a democracy built upon self-evident truth. As already noted, this proposition is recited in our Declaration but only when its meaning is seen as derived from an intellectual lineage that is far older than the Declaration itself, is the proposition compatible with faith. These are not self-evident truths known by man's initiative alone or of his own reason, but reason shaped by the hand of God. As the Apostle Paul writes in Romans 2:14-15, "What the law requires is written on [our] hearts, while [our] conscience also bears witness. . . ." The linkage between what we know as self-evidently true and God is repeated by Augustine and later by St. John of Damascus in the 700's.[14] Similarly, Aquinas writes in the middle ages:

> The precepts, therefore, contained in the Decalogue are those the knowledge of which man has in himself from God. They are such as can be known straightway from first general principles . . . and those which are known immediately from divinely infused faith. . . . [T]wo kinds of precepts, the primary and the general, which being inscribed in natural reason as *self-evident*, need no further promulgation. . . .[5]

The language of self-evident truth came to Jefferson and the American democracy through Locke, but contrary to modern historical misstatement, neither Locke nor Jefferson put man at the center of truth. Both Locke and Jefferson understood man's ability to reason as a God-like faculty, but neither was so bold as to proffer that man had become God because of it. It would be foolish to do so.

How foolish? Well, think just for a minute about the following passage from the United States Supreme Court: "Every person has the right to define their own existence, their own place in the universe."[16] These words, which come from *Planned Parenthood v. Casey* do purport to put the human self, and indeed human selfishness, at the center of the universe. In these words, there is no moral reality, no self-evident truth, no divine law creating human nature, there is only that which we want. And that which we want becomes modernly that which we claim as a right.

Inalienable Right

This brings me to the second necessary condition for the compatibility of faith and democracy. Our government is founded upon not want disguised as right, but upon *inalienable* right. An inalienable right is not that which we can sell or trade, or tragically in modern day, abort. God as man's creator has endowed each person with inalienable right as a matter of human personhood. An American democracy is thus only compatible with faith if government remains faithful to its duty to "secure these rights." And government can remain faithful to this duty only when Americans understand their own personal responsibility to live their lives for God.

In an American democracy compatible with faith, no person, and certainly no government policy, can allow or encourage others to "degrade the image of God."[17] The image of God is degraded in another by murder or serious crimes to the person, theft or other trespasses. The murderer, the thief, the abortionist, presumes to take the place of God in his victim's life, and in so doing, makes himself a false idol, a false God. One writer put this well: "Men's inalienable duties toward God translate into inalienable rights between men. God gave and commands life, liberty, property and a life of blessedness or happiness for man."[18] In short, *man has inalienable rights in our American democracy but only so long as he keeps his inalienable duties to God.* As John Paul II reminds us, "Without its Creator the creature simply disappears."[19]

Now, linking the foundational principles of the American democracy — the laws of nature, self-evident truth, and inalienable right — to an affirmation of God may suggest a disregard for the separate roles of church and state. In actuality, it is just the opposite. Only when right, truth, and the very essence of the human being are seen as outside the control of the state can the underlying purpose of separating church and state — religious freedom — be realized. If, for example, what is true can be put to majority vote, then the state crowds out the church, and the law of the state becomes a matter of dogma rather than judgment. To make sense of the religion clauses of the Constitution, one must understand the no-establishment and free exercise clauses as having a common purpose: namely, creating not a blockage to faith, but the opportunity to pursue one's own faith tradition without coercion of law.

Limited Government

Wisely, the founders of the American democracy gave preference to religious practice and belief, even as they secured against any favoritism for particular religious denominations. The preference for religion and its importance for individual discovery of truth and the personal search for the good is, of course, evidenced by the exalted placement of the First Amendment itself. More subtly, perhaps, but even more importantly, the significance of religious exercise to the pursuit of happiness in individual life is made plain in the structure of the American government. And this is the third necessary condition for compatibility between faith and democracy: a limited government.

At least on paper, the federal government is limited in function to enumerated powers; so too, states have only that power which has not be reserved to the people. Within both the federal and state governments, powers are divided, so that the chances of oppression or imposition are less. There is plentiful, and warranted, debate as to whether modern government has stayed within these intended bounds. The size of the deficit, the federal absorption of functions once performed in local community or outside of government altogether, are deeply troubling. And this is so, not merely because the marketplace might perform the job more efficiently or some other arrangement might yield greater political accountability. These factors to one side, the greatest problem posed by a bloated, centralized government is its displacement of the most important moral factors in a person's life: family and church. Each of these places can warmly and specifically explore the tenets of even denominational faith — in ways that properly are off-limits to government and sovereign force. These "first vital cells," as the Holy Father refers to them, are thus well-positioned within the natural order to put children in touch from their earliest moments of life with the instruction necessary for formation of conscience as well as responsible citizenship.

Family and church, and later in life, workplace constitute what John Courtney Murray termed the essence of our personal society or community.[20] But if government — at the federal or state level — grows too large, this society is lost, and all that remains is the individual alone and unprotected from the state.

When government assumes to direct through explicit or implicit coercion parental choice in education, the community of family, student, and teacher is lost.

When government assumes to define when life begins, the community of child and mother is lost.

When the government assumes to opine on the worth of the disabled or the elderly and infirm, the community of grandparent and grandchild is lost.

When the government dictates that those hired must have the "right" skin color or gender or ethnicity, the community of employer and employee is lost, or at least, distorted.

When the government levies high levels of taxation and establishes welfare benefits that encourage illegitimacy, the community of responsible charity and service is lost.

When the government presumes to legislate on each and every subject, especially matters of morality that in our sinful condition divide and confuse us, the critical distinction between law and morality is lost, such that the erroneous view begins to take hold that if an action is not against the law, it is morally right.

Of course in all of this, the Catholic principle of subsidiarity, which is echoed in the democratic principle of federalism, is also lost. And since by the government's own directive there is claimed a high wall of separation between church and state, the most profound loss of all is the inability of individual citizens to be guided by faith in day-to-day life. To put it bluntly, the larger the role of the state, the smaller the role for God. And here, of course, the entire American proposition, anchored — as it must be to be compatible with faith — on laws of nature, self-evident truth, and inalienable right traceable to God, unravels.

Barbarian at the Gate

Murray's response that the question of compatibility of Catholicism with American democracy was impertinent and inverted, while accurate at its core, contained a rhetorical hubris that must not obscure that Catholics are not alone in their desire to see greater compatibility between religious belief and modern democracy. Catholic, Protestant, Jew are all created in God's image and likeness. Catholic, Protestant, Jew are all inheritors of God's laws of nature, self-evident truth, and inalienable right. Murray was fully justified in fearing, however, that if this was ever forgotten, "the barbarian [would be] at the gates of the city."[21]

I believe in recent years, the cultural anxiety, if not culture war,[22] felt by Catholic, Protestant, and Jew alike has been the sighting of the barbarian at the gate. The barbarian has not yet gained complete entry, but he knocks loudly and jogs indifferently along the ellipse. We dare not let him in or complacently renew his term, for this will surely mean the incompatibility of faith and democracy in ways that may well be irreparable. In John Courtney Murray's words, faith and American democracy are compatible because we hold certain truths to be self-evident, and

> . . . we hold these truths because they are a patrimony. They are a heritage from history, through whose dark and bloody pages there runs like a silver thread the tradition of civility. . . . [And this patrimony or consensus] continually calls for public argument. The consensus is intellectual heritage; it may be lost to mind or deformed in the mind. Its final depository is the

public mind. This is indeed a perilous place to deposit what ought to be kept safe; for the public mind is exposed to corrosive rust of skepticism, to the predatory moths of deceitful [teachers], and to the incessant thieveries of forgetfulness. Therefore, the consensus can only be preserved in the public mind by argument. High argument alone will keep it alive, in the vital state of being "held."[23]

And that my fellow Catholic Americans, as I see it, is our duty to ourselves, our nation, and our God.

Endnotes

1. John Courtney Murray S.J., *We Hold These Truths* (Sheed and Ward 1960), [hereinafter WHTT], ix-x.
2. John Paul II, *Evangelium Vitae* 24, *Origins* 714, paragraph 70.
3. *Ibid.*
4. Benjamin Franklin, reprinted in Norman Cousins, *The Republic of Reason: The Personal Philosophies of the Founding Fathers* 18 (1958).
5. School District of Abington Township v. Schempp, 374 U.S. 203 (1963), 303-04.
6. Rosenberger v. Rector, 115 S.Ct. 2510 (1995); Capitol Square v. Pinette, 115 S.Ct. 2440 (1995).
7. WHTT, referencing Justice Douglas in Zorach v. Clauson, 343 U.S. 306, 313-14 (1952), 30.
8. WHTT, ix.
9. George Washington, Farewell Address, in *Documents of American History*, Vol. I (Henry S. Commager and Milton Cantor, eds., 10th ed., 1988), 173.
10. WHTT, 309.
11. John Paul II, *Veritatis Splendor*, paragraph 101 (St. Paul ed. 1992).
12. *Ibid.*
13. William Blackstone, *Commentaries*, vol. 1 (Cadell & W. Davies ed. 1803), 41-42 (First edition 1765).
14. *De Fide Orthodoxa*, reprinted in *The Nicene and Post-Nicene Fathers* (Philip Schaf and Henry Wace, eds., Eerdmans 1979).
15. Thomas Aquinas, 1 *Summa Theologica*, Q. 100, Art. 3, (University of Chicago, Great Books ed., 1990) (Original draft 1265).
16. *Planned Parenthood v. Casey*, 114 S.Ct. 909 (1994).

17. Gary Amos, *Defending The Declaration* (Wolgemuth & Hyatt 1989), 107-08.

18. *Ibid*, 108.

19. John Paul II, *Veritatis Splendor*, para. 39.

20. WHTT, 35.

21. *Ibid.*, 12.

22. For an antidote to the culture war through the teaching of virtue within the family, *see* Douglas W. Kmiec, *Cease-Fire on the Family* (Crisis Books/Notre Dame 1995).

23. WHTT, 11.

Can Catholic Americans
Be Trusted in the Public Square?

That title may strike some as anachronistic. Surely, they might say, it is an outdated question that is no longer pertinent to our day, or to the Catholic Campaign's call for a vibrant Catholic participation in American public life. After all, we do not live in a time when the Know-Nothing Party and other anti-Catholic bigots charged that Catholics owed their loyalty to an alien power — a power that taught that "error has no rights," and declared the political ideal of a "Catholic state in a Catholic society."

Such anti-Catholic suspicion, we might think, was a long time ago. Surely Catholic Americans have demonstrated over these two hundred years that they are loyal citizens, that their success in America is more than matched by their contributions to America, that they are prepared, when necessary, to seal their pledge to freedom by the shedding of their patriot blood. All this is true enough.

In fact, it has been observed that Catholics, especially those coming from the great immigrations of the last century, have tended to be super-patriots, so eager have they been to demonstrate their Americanism. In the years since the Council, many Catholics have boasted that they are now just like everybody else in America. It is not at all clear that this is something to be proud of.

We hear it said frequently that there is a peculiarly American way of being Catholic. It is usually added that the big problem in the Church is that Rome doesn't understand that. Those who speak that way emphasize that they are *American* Catholics. The great challenge for the years ahead, however, is to demonstrate not that we are American Catholics but that we are *Catholic* Americans

— meaning that there is a distinctively Catholic way of being American.

That challenge comes with a risk. The risk is that people will once again ask whether Catholics can be trusted in the democratic public square. In 1984, when John O'Connor arrived as Archbishop of New York, the Institute on Religion and Public Life held a number of dinners for him to meet with various leadership sectors in the city. You will recall that that was the year when a vice-presidential candidate took it upon herself to present a rather eccentric view of Catholic teaching on abortion. The new Archbishop responded with a public statement clearly setting forth the Church's teaching on the matter. This caused an enormous furor, with editorials railing against the Archbishop for "interfering" in politics and "violating the separation of church and state."

The controversy came up at one of these dinners, at which one of the most influential editors in the country said, "Archbishop, when John F. Kennedy was elected in 1960, some of us thought that the question had been answered whether you Catholics really belong here, whether you understand how we do things around here. But I must tell you frankly, Archbishop, that in the short time you've been in New York some of us are beginning to ask that question again."

"That question" has two parts: Whether we belong here, and whether we understand how they do things around here. The implication is that we do not really belong unless we understand — *and agree with* — how things are done around here. American Catholics might go along with that implication; Catholic Americans will not. We know that we belong here; there is no question about that. But, inspired by the bold leadership of such as Cardinal O'Connor, we also know that we belong in America in order to change the way things have been done for far too long in America. Bringing about that change is, as I understand it, the heart of the mission of the Catholic Campaign for America.

Moral Renewal

Catholics are by no means alone in working for such change — in working for nothing less than the moral renewal of what the founders of this country called the American experiment in ordered liberty. On the most fevered question in our public life — who belongs to the community for which we accept common responsibility? — it seemed for a long time that Catholics were alone in contending that unborn children belong to that community. But today, thank God, in the abortion struggle we are joined by growing legions of other Christians — especially by evangelical Protestants — but also by many Jews and those who profess no religion. There is a truly ecumenical convergence in the confident determination that we can, and by the grace of God we will, turn back the encroaching "culture of death."

While we should judiciously cooperate with various alliances and coalitions, Catholics have a most particular responsibility. By virtue of our numbers, by virtue of the richness of our tradition, and by virtue of our worldwide communion with bishops in communion with the Bishop of Rome — who is Peter among us — ours is a distinctive responsibility and ours a singular role to play. If the Catholic Church is what she claims to be — and she is — she cannot be subsumed under any movement or cause or coalition or ideology, no matter how attractive. To those who would recruit the Church for the advancement of their agenda, whether they be of the left or of the right, we must lovingly but firmly say: The Bride of Christ is not for hire.

Surely our Bishops are right when they say that, in the everyday give and take of politics, the Church must be nonpartisan. And surely we must share their regret when on so many questions their official statements are perceived as scrupulously nonpartisan on the side of the Democratic party. We are assured that that is not their intention, and of course that assurance must be accepted. The Bishops have acknowledged their problem of working through a burdensome bureaucracy — a bureaucracy that is astute at "reading the signs of the times," but of late seems to be reading the signs of yesterday, which is to say the editorial page of *The New York Times* of today.

But the teaching of the Council is clear that the primary Catholic voice in the political give-and-take of the public square must be the voice of the Catholic laity. As the Bishops put it in their "Political Responsibility" statement for 1966: "It is the laity who are primarily responsible for activity in political affairs, since they have the major responsibility for renewal of the temporal order."

Catholic Americans who are determined to play their full part in our public life, who are determined to change the way things are done around here, will form alliances with others, and will strengthen such alliances by being unapologetically Catholic. I might even say by being proudly Catholic, but pride is a sin. It is not with pride but with gratitude that we can point to the singular role Catholics have played in restoring a measure of moral sanity to a world gone mad. To cite but one obvious example, there would today be no pro-life movement in America or in the world were it not for the Catholic Church. In resisting euthanasia, in the defense of the radically handicapped, in the restoration of sexuality worthy of human beings made in the image of God, in securing for parents the right to direct the education of their children — on these and a host of other questions Catholics bring to bear a doctrine divinely revealed and tested through the centuries by the faith and life of the Catholic people.

Catholics may sympathize with the conservatisms that come and go in the public square, but such conservatisms are all passing novelties as compared with the Church's great conservation of moral truth. It is *that* conservative movement — the Catholic Church itself — that claims our utmost devotion, for it bears the truth from the past that points us with utmost confidence to the future.

Consider where we are at the end of the twentieth century, at the edge of the third millennium. At the end of this slum of a century — this century in which ideological madnesses have piled up mountains of corpses and loosed rivers of blood — there is on the stage of world history only one message and one messenger that speaks a compelling word of hope. The message is, "Be not afraid!" And the messenger is Pope John Paul II. Wherein lies the authority with which he speaks? How to explain why the world is turning its tear-stained face to this old man, this son of the grief-drenched soil of Poland? Surely it is because he is the messenger of the One who is both *the* messenger and the message, the crucified and risen Christ.

"Be not afraid!" — so says Our Lord and so says His faithful servant, John Paul II. Be not afraid to cross the threshold of hope. Be not afraid to cross the threshold of the third millennium with the flag of faith unfurled. Do not hesitate at the threshold, filled with fear and doubt. "He has gone ahead of you into Galilee," the Easter angel announced to the terrified disciples. And so the Holy Father says to a dispirited and terrified world: Christ is going ahead of you into the third millennium. Follow him. Be not afraid to step from the shadow of your fears to cross the threshold into the sunlight of hope. To a world enthralled to the culture of death, comes One who has returned from the dead to announce the *Evangelium Vitae*, the Gospel of Life.

A Public Faith

This, then, is the faith and this the truth that emboldens Catholic Americans in every dimension of their discipleship, and not least in their public determination to change the way things are done around here. In American public life, such faith and such truth is deeply troubling to many. As with the editor who challenged the man whom I am pleased to call my bishop, it makes them wonder whether Catholics really belong here. It's fine to have faith, they say, but don't you understand that you should keep it to yourself? And as for truth, well, perhaps there is such a thing, but don't you understand that in a democracy all truths are equal? And don't you understand that the separation of church and state

49

means that the public square must be kept free of religion and religiously-grounded morality? Don't you understand, in sum, that this is a secular society?

We should listen respectfully, and then say as clearly as possible: No, we do not understand any of those things. We understand that that is the way you think things are, and that is the way you think things should be done around here; we understand that that is the way things have been done around here for a long time. But what you don't understand, we must say, is that we, along with millions of other Americans, have determined that we are not going to do things that way anymore. We are going to do things the old-fashioned way, the way the founders of this country envisioned they should be done.

We believe with the founders that truth is not the enemy but the best friend of freedom. We believe with the founders that this great experiment is premised upon truth — as in "We hold these truths to be self-evident. . . ." We believe with the founders that the separation of church and state does not mean and cannot mean the separation of religion from public life. On the contrary, the very idea of the limited state requires the acknowledgment of a higher sovereignty. As in the founders' appeal to "Nature and Nature's God." As in the pledge of allegiance to "One nation under God." And so we say to those who distrust us that we understand them very well. Now it is time for them to understand; it is time for them to understand again, or maybe for the first time, the truths by which this American experiment was launched and by which alone it can be sustained in the future.

The great question is truth, including moral truth. Not simply moral truth in our personal lives — as critically important as that is — but moral truth in our public life. The truth about freedom is that there is no freedom apart from truth. This is the argument advanced by the Holy Father in his 1991 encyclical, *Centesimus Annus* (The Hundredth Year). Writing in support of liberal democracy, he contends that democracy cannot be sustained apart from the truth about freedom:

Today there is a tendency to claim that agnosticism and skeptical relativism are the philosophy and basic attitude which correspond to democratic forms of political life. Those who are convinced that they know the truth and firmly adhere to it are considered unreliable from a democratic point of view, since they do not accept that truth is determined by the majority, or that it is subject to variation according to different political trends. It must be observed in this regard that if there is no ultimate truth to guide and direct political activity, then ideas and convictions can easily be manipulated for reasons of power. As history demonstrates, a democracy without moral truth easily turns into open or thinly disguised totalitarianism.

New Order for the Ages

It is not too much to say that the way things have been done around here for the last fifty years and more were leading us in the direction of a "thinly disguised totalitarianism." The naked public square, the refusal to acknowledge a sovereignty higher than the state, resulted in a government of unbounded ambition to control more and more of the life of society. A perverse reading of the separation of church and state meant that, wherever the government advanced, religion must retreat — and the government was advancing almost everywhere. The same perverse reading meant that the deepest moral convictions of the people, grounded as they are in religion, must be excluded from public deliberation and decision. Although promoted in the name of democracy, this claim is profoundly anti-democratic. It is in fact a thinly disguised totalitarianism, and, if not resisted, it can well end up in totalitarianism without disguise.

But now we see evidence of a new determination to do things differently around here. Maybe we will start doing things the old-fashioned way, which is the way of the future. The founders called this experiment a *novus ordo seclorum* — a new order for the ages. That is perhaps saying too much. No order is forever, except the order of the one, holy, catholic, and apostolic Church. But, whatever the fortunes of this American experiment, the future belongs to the spirit of freedom. And that is because human beings were created for freedom, and freedom can only be secured by the truth. "You will know the truth, and the truth will make you free." This is a theme repeated again and again, like a trip-hammer, throughout this pontificate. I think it likely that two generations from now, like Popes Leo and Gregory before him, this Pope will be known as John Paul the Great. And when they reach for the phrase that best describes his greatness, they will call him "The Pope of Freedom."

Seldom in two thousand years has there been a teaching pontificate of such energy and intellectual persuasiveness. Consider only the most recent encyclicals. *Centesimus Annus*: Nowhere else in the world is to be found such a comprehensive and convincing account of what makes for a free and virtuous society. *Veritatis Splendor*: The splendor of the truth worth dying for that makes life, now and forever, worth living for. *Evangelium Vitae*: The Gospel of Life addressed to a world infatuated with death. *Ut Unum Sint:* Calling us to act in obedience to the prayer of Our Lord that "they may all be one," so that the unity of Christians becomes a sign of the promised unity of humankind. These four documents alone present the world with an ensemble of reasons to hope, of reasons to believe, of reasons to act, of reasons not to be afraid. There is nothing else even remotely like this teaching in the whole of the world.

The teaching of the Magisterium equips the Catholic laity to assume their rightful role in giving voice to moral truth in our public life. And yet some of our fellow Americans worry that we are trying to impose our truth upon them. We have the duty of trying to understand why they worry about that. In the words of *Redemptoris Missio* (The Mission of the Redeemer) we must assure them, "The Church imposes nothing, she only proposes." The truth about truth is that truth cannot be imposed. This year is the thirtieth anniversary of *Dignitatis Humanae*, the Council's great Declaration on Religious Freedom. The declaration teaches, "The truth cannot impose itself except by virtue of its own truth, as it makes its entrance into the mind at once quietly and with power." "The Church imposes nothing, she only proposes." But what a proposal! We Catholic Americans are chosen for this moment to demonstrate in our personal lives and to propose in the public square the truth that makes and keeps us free. To those who have been in charge of how things were done around here, to those who fear the revitalization of American democracy that is now underway, Catholic Americans say, "Be not afraid." Be not afraid to listen to the truth, be not afraid to engage the truth, be not afraid to trust the truth. For finally, nothing can be trusted but the truth.

A Call to Holiness

There are many far better equipped than I to teach about holiness. The only meaningful credential I bring to this topic is that of being human. Very human. As such, I am painfully aware of the many times and varied ways that I have failed to even hear, much less respond to, the call to holiness.

So, my gift this morning is only a modest one for it comes wrapped in the brokenness of my life. And yet, it is through this very woundedness that I have come to believe I have a unique gift to share. I recognized the value of my gift the moment I could fully identify with those Our Lord was tenderly addressing when He said, "For I came not to call the righteous, but sinners" (Mt 9:13).

It is as a grateful member of the Catholic Church, a body of imperfect gift givers, that I have managed to push aside enough fear to address this topic. How true it is that Satan tries to engage us at our point of greatest fear. For me, that fear took the ominous shape of ridicule in response to a public witness that would necessarily be hopelessly flawed and fragile.

And then I came across a passage written by Saint Francis de Sales almost five hundred years ago:

> As soon as the children of this world perceive that you desire to
> follow a devout life, they will shoot at you a thousand arrows of
> mockery and detraction. The most malicious will calumniate
> your change as being hypocrisy, bigotry, and artifice. They will
> say that the world has frowned upon you and that being rejected
> by it, you turn to God (*Introduction to the Devout Life*).

If finding the courage to speak honestly and openly still posed a problem, it no longer could once I read the unambiguous directive of Our Lord Himself, "So every one who acknowledges me before men, I also will acknowledge before my Father who is in heaven; but whoever denies me before men, I also will deny before my Father who is in heaven" (Mt 10:32-33).

And so it is with a renewed appreciation that discipleship is not for the fainthearted or those who attach too much importance on being accepted that I shall now try to shed light on this topic of paramount importance to each of us.

What Holiness Is Not

No discussion about holiness can proceed very far without first reaching an agreement about what "holiness" is and what it is *not*. Over the past few months, I have listened to many well-intentioned friends stammer their way through some rather peculiar definitions of the word. Most of these definitions, relied upon vague notions of virtue cast in ethereal images far removed from what you or I would call everyday life. Some were as rigid as a gilded icon and as cold as a marble statue and did little to offer practical insight into the kind of holiness that could be lived out in a competitive workplace, a frenzied checkout line, or around a crowded family-room table. Considering this basic confusion, it is small wonder that so many admit to a basic discomfort with the subject altogether, much less anyone who measures up to such distorted perceptions of the word.

Why do we insist upon removing holiness from the blood, sweat, and tears of daily life? How can holiness come alive in and through our living, breathing actions if we deny it a pulse and relegate its domain to the past lives of saints or an elite few who are trying to achieve spiritual excellence in our world today?

We might benefit from asking ourselves whether our restrictions are a symptom of misguided humility, a lack of creativity, or a particularly virulent strain of self-deception. Let's take a moment to consider each and, if necessary, try to correct all three.

Misguided Humility

What form of humility can afford to overlook the all-inclusive passage in the Gospel of St. John when he writes, "God so loved the world that he gave his only Son, that *whoever* believes in him should not perish but have eternal life" (Jn 3:16). Has our faith become so weak, so selective that we doubt whether the redemptive process was intended for us too? This is surely not the kind of humility that St. Benedict so passionately proscribed for us but a dangerous imitation — the sort of flimsy look-alike that the "master of lies" would delight in our adopting. If any of us have accepted this artificial brand of humility, we must dismiss its destructive agenda before it can silence our call to holiness with debilitating guilt and overwhelming despair.

Lack of Creativity

What chance is there that the limitations we have placed on holiness may have to do with a woeful lack of creativity in trying to apply seemingly antiquated principles of goodness to our darkened culture? We might return for enlightenment to that same passage in St. John's Gospel where he writes, "For God sent the Son into the world, not to condemn the world, but that the world might be saved through him" (Jn 3:17). We can find further hope in the fact that the world John is referring to is the same one that Our Lord is speaking of when He adds a time frame to His promise: "I am with you *always*, to the close of the age" (Mt 28:20).

I find no evidence of any period of history being excluded — no matter how advanced or depraved its culture may have become. To the contrary, I find many, many references to the universal and unchanging role of the "chosen ones" as the "children of God," who are to continue in Our Lord's redemptive work by tirelessly living lives that are "holy and pleasing to God." If we have been only lukewarm in our efforts to find new relevance in the timeless call to holiness, then we must strengthen our resolve to bring greater creativity and determination to this most vital process.

Self-deception

Let's consider the third possible culprit that could be separating us from a more realistic idea of holiness: self-deception. By definition, this will be the most difficult problem to diagnose. In trying to discern if our discomfort has anything to do with fooling ourselves, it may be worth noting what a convenient excuse an unrealistically high moral standard can provide. After all, the more readily we can dismiss a goal as an "impossible dream," the more easily we can absolve ourselves from any responsibility to try to achieve it. Even the most meager, sporadic attempts to measure up will find a ready-made explanation for their inevitable failure. We cannot afford to leave any room for this type of mind game if we are to graduate to a more authentic response to the call to holiness.

What Holiness Is

We need only to spend a few minutes trying to instruct a child in the true meaning of holiness to grasp the importance of simplicity in any definition. Similarly, those of us who have spent time in business have learned that the best mission statements are those that are kept clear and concise. Since our goal today is not just to describe but to inspire to action, I have chosen a definition of holiness that I believe has the greatest chance of accomplishing both. It is captured in the unassuming title of a fifteenth-century manuscript reported to be the most popular book after the Bible. The text is named *The Imitation of Christ*.

In these pages, we are reminded by Thomas à Kempis that the only sure path to holiness is the one that follows in the footsteps of Our Lord. And those footsteps, while both human and divine, were anything but removed from the turbulence and joy, the agony and the ecstasy of everyday life.

To imitate "The Word Made Flesh," the Christ who assumed human form, we must recognize Him in the breaking of His body as much as the breaking of the bread. How else can we hope to imitate Christ unless we are willing to see His hands comforting the grieving widow, healing the outcast leper, blessing the repentant sinner? How can we possibly try to walk in His footsteps if we're afraid to draw in close — to touch His wounded hands, wipe His sweaty face, anoint His dusty feet? How can we even begin to hear His call if we cannot hear His voice patiently answering the Pharisees, gently forgiving His murderers, wisely dismissing the stone throwers?

Ours is not the religion of a clever prophet who kept a safe distance from the messy, unpredictable action of life, but one who engaged in relationships as diverse and complex as any we could ever experience today. He did not leave us with a simple, well-crafted story line or ten cold, stone tablets with which to piece together holiness. Rather, He gave us Himself, a living testimony to the true meaning of holiness as we are called to experience it in the anguish and the glory of everyday life.

How Important Is the Call

Before trying to figure out how we might better answer this call, it is worth spending a few moments establishing how important the call to holiness is. It could reasonably be said that a call is only as important as its author. In this case, the Source is our Creator or God Himself. He gave us His Son in human form and asked us to follow Him. In the first book of Peter, the call to imitate Christ could not have been made more clear, "But as he who called you is holy, be holy yourselves in all your conduct; since it is written, 'You shall be holy, for I am holy' " (1 Pt 1:15-16).

Another way of assessing the significance of the call is to consider how much emphasis it is given in sacred Scripture which, after all, we refer to as "the Word of God." Holiness, in one form or another, is mentioned over six hundred times in the Bible and the entire book of Leviticus is devoted to this subject!

We can also learn something of its paramount importance by

referring to one of the many specific passages that causally connect holiness with salvation. Let's turn to the one in Hebrews that leaves no doubt about either what is expected of us or the consequences of our failure to obey, "Strive . . . for the holiness without which no one will see the Lord" (Heb 12:14). To summarize, it would be no exaggeration to state that holiness is the primary purpose for our very existence.

How to Answer the Call

If we are willing to admit the singular importance of this call to holiness and we are comfortable with "the imitation of Christ" as our working definition, then we must now come to grips with what this way of life is likely to entail. As one of His many followers who has found the message of Easter to be much easier to embrace than that of Good Friday, it is time to address the single biggest obstacle that most of us will face on our path to holiness. Thomas à Kempis was hinting at it when he wrote, "Jesus has many lovers of heaven, but He has few bearers of His Cross." I'm speaking, of course, about suffering — *all* human suffering: from the seemingly petty little disappointment that mildly disrupts our daily routine to the crushing, life-altering defeat that absorbs every ounce of our energy just to survive it.

The Role of Suffering

Suffering is the crucible for anyone who would answer "yes" to the call to holiness. For each moment of pain presents a critical choice: whether to interpret its impact as an opportunity for grace — or an excuse for despair. A gift or a burden? This is what distinguishes the sincere follower of Christ from the phony imposter.

Our role model Himself made His criteria for holiness perfectly clear, "If any man would come after me, let him deny himself and take up his cross and follow me" (Mt 16:24). This is why so much of Thomas à Kempis's writing about the imitation of Christ focuses on the absolute necessity of freeing ourselves from "all inordinate affections," from "all earthly things that are transitory and shortly passing away." With prophetic insight for our own day and age, he warns us "not to cling to them too much, lest you be seized with love of them and so perish in the end." Renunciation of worldly pleasures and suffering, this is the bitter medicine, the spiritual vitamins prescribed by the greatest saints to fortify us. How else can we learn to "bear our suffering more cheerfully" and "submit ourselves wholly to God's Will?" (Thomas à Kempis).

The Blessed Mother's Example

Whenever we speak of humble submission to divine will, our thoughts naturally turn to the human being who did best at this exercise; the one whose "soul magnified the Lord." For those who are serious about imitating Christ, the Blessed Mother provides the most valuable of gifts: *magnification* of her Son's example. Her life presents the ideal canvas on which to view what perfect holiness is all about in all of its hues and dimensions.

Two Scenes From Her Life

We need only to visit two memorable scenes from her exemplary life to recognize what a leading part suffering played throughout her earthly existence. Let's consider that most tender and vulnerable of moments in a woman's life — the moment when she learns for the first time that she is pregnant. How often, when I am counseling one of the hundreds of lonely, frightened, embarrassed women who turn to The Nurturing Network for help each year, my thoughts return to this young Jewish girl named Mary who, two thousand years ago, learned firsthand about the acute suffering and personal sacrifice of a crisis pregnancy. And I wonder why we deny ourselves the chance to understand her better as an authentic human being by skipping over those highly charged, intense moments that must have occurred between the Angel Gabriel's startling announcement and Our Lady's humble acceptance.

My guess is that precisely the same tortured thoughts that we hear each day in the counseling offices of The Nurturing Network raced through her brilliant, perceptive mind: "What will Joseph think? . . . How could I handle his leaving me? . . . How will I ever explain this to my parents? They'll be so ashamed! . . . What if the neighbors find out? I can't put my family through this." In fact, the only anguishing fear I can think of that she may not have had to endure is whether some ambitious journalist would try to advance his career by sullying her reputation! Suffice it to say, this scene in all of its eventual glory, had a prologue filled with pain.

Let's turn to another scene that we may have drained from any color and deprived of relevance for our lives. Mary was, perhaps more than anything else, a mother. Have you ever stopped to consider what this gentle Lady must have experienced the morning *after* the crucifixion? Her Son, after all, had not been afforded a dignified, private tribunal or even a discreet, quiet execution. No, her Son had been accused in the most public of forums of a political crime punishable by death! My guess is that people talked. A lot. Gossip and rash judgment were probably as much a part of the social dance of her time as they are today.

And, being "free from sin" does not mean that she did not wake up with the taste of rage in her mouth. Can you picture her managing to get dressed that morning and walk into the marketplace for the day's food? Do you see the faces of the townspeople? The knowing glances, the looks of disapproval, the sudden detours to avoid having to talk. Can you hear their whispers? "I told you she was way too lax with Him; nowhere near enough discipline when He was growing up!" "She and Joseph were obviously too busy with their own interests; they didn't spend enough time when He was young. She could have prevented all of this."

Suffice it to say, the Blessed Mother knew what pain felt like; she and suffering were intimate friends. And so, if her example is to aid us in our attempt to learn more about how to imitate her Son, it will have much to do with imitating her courageous and humble acceptance of each and every sacrifice in a spirit of good will.

Why the Cross? Why Suffering?

Again and again we are reminded throughout sacred Scripture that the path to holiness *necessarily* passes by way of the cross. Still, you might well ask, why the cross was given such a pivotal role to play in Our Lord's redemptive mission? For that matter, why must suffering and pain continue to play such a major part in our own call to holiness? These are surely the questions many of us will have at the top of our list when we meet Almighty God face to face. They are as persistent and perplexing as, "Why war? Why sickness? Why famine? Why injustice? Why poverty? Why death?"

The greatest minds throughout history have pondered these same questions with no definitive answers. And yet, we may come closest to at least the rough outline of a good answer when we reflect honestly upon our very nature as human beings. For unlike Christ and His Blessed Mother, we know that our lives are marked by original sin. Every day most of us give fresh new meaning to Our Lord's phrase, "The spirit indeed is willing, but the flesh is weak" (Mt 26:41).

This is the reason given most often for the cross: so that we might be saved by His suffering and physical death. We are told in the letter to the Hebrews, "We have been sanctified through the offering of the body of Jesus Christ. . ." (Heb 10:10). And yet, we know that this same merciful Savior *could* have redeemed us by just one drop of His precious blood, or for that matter, during any one of the awesome miracles He performed throughout His earthly life. And so, we still find ourselves wondering, "Why the cross?"

Why did He elect this pain-filled, tear-stained plot in order to make His message of salvation known to the world? Why did He wait for the precise moment when His physical body appeared to be weakest and His earthly career most shattered to perform His greatest miracle?

In order to answer this tantalizing question, let's consider what our task of imitating Christ would have been like if He had chosen *not* to take on the unpleasant, painful part of the human experience. What if He had opted to *leave out* of His life story the agony of anticipating death alone in a garden, the calculating betrayal of a close friend, the frustrating injustice of a kangaroo court, the heart-wrenching humiliation of a jeering crowd, the physical torture of a Roman scourging, the total anguish of a public crucifixion? In fact, what if our divine Savior had decided *not* to "partake of the cup" of suffering and, instead, had selected for His final exit scene a magnificent victory celebration complete with cheering crowds and converted enemies?

Would any part of this scene have guided or strengthened us the next time we felt tempted to hide like Peter, doubt like Thomas, or cheat like Judas? Where would we look for inspiration the next time we felt justified in keeping more than our fair share or hating our enemies or getting even with those who harm us? Where would we find any meaningful basis for interpreting that most ultimate of paradoxes, the one that separates "the wheat from the chaff" and the "called from the chosen": "He who finds his life will lose it; and he who loses his life for my sake will find it" (Mt 10:39).

The short answer is that without Our Lord's courageous example of suffering in all of its concrete and tangible forms, we would have been lost in our effort to live lives "holy and pleasing to God." If we have difficulty "walking in His footsteps" even with the benefit of His powerful example, we wouldn't have had a chance of succeeding without it.

And so, let's conclude our discussion of suffering by fully acknowledging the critical role it plays in enabling us to reach our goal of salvation. Let's thank God for being a wise and loving Father who, after counting every hair on our heads, knows full well that we desperately need the example of His Son in order to answer our own personal call to holiness. And, finally, let's even consider a change in attitude the next time we are tempted to "curse the darkness" or lighten our load when suffering comes our way. Perhaps it is time to hear a familiar voice gently "calling to us by name" and inviting us to know His Son more intimately through whatever we are asked to sacrifice in this world.

Conclusion

Before concluding, it might be helpful to briefly review our progress. We have gained considerable insight and comfort from working with the simplest definition of holiness, "the imitation of Christ." Through the inspiring examples of the Blessed Mother and Our Lord Himself, we have deepened our appreciation for the unique and powerful invitation to grace that all suffering provides. We understand more fully that since Our Lord's life was marked so profoundly by suffering and sacrifice, the more perfect our imitation of Him becomes, the more ours, too, will necessarily include suffering and sacrifice. We recognize that the call to holiness is for everyone, without exception, and that it can often be best heard when we adopt the honest stance of a humble, repentant sinner. Finally, we understand the paramount importance of this call to holiness, given its divine origin and most ultimate of spiritual consequences.

In closing, I am reminded of one of my favorite responsorial psalms, "If today you hear His voice, harden not your hearts." His call can be heard in the lonely wail of a grieving parent, or the bombastic remark of a teenage child; in the timid invitation of an estranged relative, or the inconvenient phone call of a fair-weather friend; in the plaintive call for help of an alcoholic neighbor or the caustic, not-so-passing comment of a discouraged spouse.

For as we have shared, the call to holiness is neither abstract nor something that can be postponed for our next retreat. Its challenge is here and now, at this precise moment. This is when and where the imitation of Christ becomes real. For the waitress who pours the water, the speaker who shares a few thoughts, or the person sitting right beside you — the one with the furrowed brow, perhaps nervously fidgeting with the napkin or wiping away a tear or catching a much-needed nap. This is where and how the call to holiness can best be heard . . . and with a reward that echoes down through the ages from generation to generation, "As you did it to one of the least of these my brethren, you did it to me" (Mt 25:40).

The Role of Catholic Women
in Building a Culture of Life

The contribution of women to society in any century is
inestimable and noble, as is that of men, especially if it is informed
by spiritual values that strive for the best that human beings can
be. But that contribution becomes even more important when the
culture changes and takes a negative turn, as ours has done. Today
women are well-educated, serving as professionals, as politicians,
as prime ministers. Women have the talent to *do* anything. But at
the end of the twentieth century, we are living through a cultural
crisis that adversely affects our ideas about fundamental values,
cheapening the value of human life and even questioning what it is
to be a woman. Some would redefine the meaning of womanhood
as a reality that is autonomous, anti-child, and anti-gender.
Catholic women have a vital role to play in defending a culture
based on truth, including the intrinsic value of motherhood, the
complementarity of the relationship of women and men, and
especially in restoring the power of spiritual living and self-
sacrifice inspired by the example of Mary, Mother of God and the
first Christian.

Good Versus Evil

The dramatic changes in our culture are affecting the way
women see themselves and their role. We are living through a
period of cultural change that has many negative factors, a
lessening of moral virtue, perhaps the breakup of Western culture
as we have known it. The Holy Father says in *Evangelium Vitae*
that "This situation, with its lights and shadows, ought to make us

all fully aware that we are facing an enormous and dramatic clash between good and evil, death and life, the 'culture of death' and the 'culture of life.' We find ourselves not only 'faced with' but necessarily 'in the midst of' this conflict."[1] We can safely assume that this cultural clash will be with us as we enter the new millennium, and so our reflection on the role of women must be deep enough to be a sure guide for many years.

The culture of death in our country has influenced the women's movement as evidenced by their enshrining the right to abortion as the number one women's right. The Supreme Court allows women to choose to take the life of another human being for any reason during the first nine months of life after conception. Not all feminists are comfortable with this priority, and that gives reason for hope. But a culture that endorses an attitude of efficiency over solidarity and, as the Holy Father says, is headed toward barbarism. Human life that does not meet certain standards is considered disposable, especially the unborn, or the elderly, or those who are in any way a burden. The powerful have lined up against the weak in what he calls a "conspiracy against life" reaching beyond the bounds of personal and family life to international relations.[2] Some say we are becoming two nations, one with a traditional outlook and one permissive. My husband is writing a book about this, the title of which is "Slouching Towards Gomorrah," which tells you where he thinks it is going. He has hired a contractor to start building catacombs in the backyard!

The Pope has questioned whether or not democracy can last if it is not based on fundamental truths, especially regard for the dignity of human life. This must be of concern to all Catholics, but women have a special role to play in keeping track of those trends which are harmful to a culture of life.

The Uniqueness of Women

Women have to counteract the especially harmful views of women and family that have become dominant in the culture and cannot be ignored. We face a cultural ferment in which an array of gender feminists shudder at the idea of women's uniqueness; after all, equality is what women are after and to talk about uniqueness implies difference and even complementarity. They see uniqueness as a chauvinistic idea. Other women go into a rage at the suggestion that this uniqueness could have anything to do with biology. As Bella Abzug said at the U.N., "We will not be forced back into the 'biology is destiny' concept that seeks to define, confine, and reduce women and girls to their physical sexual characteristics."[3] Gender is no longer tied to sex. It is evolving into ever new socially constructed roles and manifestations, such as lesbianism and transsexuality. This is the view of reality they want to impose through government programs and women's groups.

These views were very much at play at the U.N. Conference on Women in Beijing, the largest gathering of women in history, and the latest episode in the ongoing struggle over which of these views will prevail. There we saw the most recent concerted effort by radical feminists to repudiate the role of woman as mother and to demand equality through government programs. Feminists know that the American people will not give them a hearing on many of their ideas, so they are using international forums like the U.N. and International Planned Parenthood to legitimize their ideas and gain a following. This time they did not get all that they wanted. Forty countries filed reservations on various aspects of the final document, and that means they did not achieve the consensus needed to call the meeting a success.

One feminist gain was sexual rights for women, a term that was not defined in the final document. "Sexual rights" are like the amorphous "right to privacy." Since no one knows what it means, the term can be "used" and expanded as needed. The term "sexual rights" itself demonstrates a selective use of rights language that, as Mary Ann Glendon, head of the Vatican delegation, says, is a "troubling trend" because it moves away from the tradition of universal human rights for all people. It is part of a trend of aggrieved groups to promote their agendas by inventing new rights. One hopeful sign was that pro-life and religiously motivated women were better represented than at any U.N. conference, and that is a significant development. Our presence must continue at meetings at home and abroad. By defending the institutions we consider basic to society from the negative influences of a liberalism gone wild, we are setting forth the truth that many women have never heard, and slowly, person by person, building a culture of life.

Our Christian understanding of authentic womanhood is the only sure foundation for the future of society. That understanding of woman and of the human person is rooted in truth. Women are the carriers of culture, and that is why the feminist assault on the ideas of the family and sexuality are destroying society, especially the family, and belittling the lives of traditionally-minded women. We have to counteract this force by trying to convince feminists they are wrong about gender only being socially constructed, about equality, and about seeking freedom apart from moral authority. That is done by argument, discussion, and living example that faith and moral virtue make a difference for the better in our lives.

Areas Women Must Influence

Creating a "culture of life" is a work of love and therefore more than a political reality. It is essentially human culture that "answers man's spiritual and moral needs."[4] The family is at the heart of this culture of love providing the best place for the growth and development of human beings and their happiness.

We live in a society that has enshrined in its law a right to kill innocent human life, a situation that we must eventually change if we are ever to continue as a free and just society. At the heart of America is this wound that will not go away. We act as a restraining hand to those who would do harm to innocent life, especially those who cannot speak for themselves, especially tiny unborn human beings. This work puts us at the front lines of the culture war.

A second related area for women's influence is a positive view of the complementarity of men and women. This view informs all of Catholic social teaching and is in the process of being ridiculed by the cultural elites. Gender feminism has had a deleterious effect on relations between men and women, especially among the younger generation. Young men do not know how to talk or act with many young women. A man does not know if he should pay for lunch or hold open a door, because the woman may consider his gesture chauvinistic and not respectful of her independence. Feminists are suspicious of all male intentions in personal relations, marriage, business, and science. Discussion of women's roles and women's relation to man has become politicized. Instead of a national discussion of how women and men can work together for a better society, feminists claim that women are an oppressed group and need new rights in order to achieve true equality. Men are made to feel that they are oppressors, and even useless.

Women Are Not Victims

We should not fall into the trap of being labeled as groups of victims and oppressors. This kind of thinking obscures the true identity of men and women, which is rooted not in ideology but in anthropology. Women and men are individuals first, with many gifts and talents whose mutual relationship and working together will build up the common good of society and the family. Just at the point when women are poised to do great things (and are doing great things) the public conversation has become very politically correct and even uncivil. A delegate speaking recently in defense of motherhood at the U.N. brought a response of laughter. Into this conversation we have to bring the sanity and truth of the Catholic tradition by not defining woman's role in opposition to that of men but as one of complementarity. Our view of life is the biblical view which now must be defended. To put it positively, we have to articulate our belief about authentic womanhood, a role that many of us live, against a push from feminists to see women as autonomous persons who can do whatever they wish. It is a challenging task when the underlying assumptions of all of our efforts are ridiculed and de-constructed by people with little concern for the truth. Presenting the Catholic position on these matters in the public forum will throw light on the confusion that reigns in many minds, and is another contribution to building a culture of life. The great spiritual void created by postmodernism is being filled by a reversion to paganism and ways of thinking and acting that do not promote life and happiness but rather promote a culture of death.

Ours is a fundamentally different approach. We see women and men as created in the image and likeness of God by a loving Creator God. God, as it were, sent us a message in the fact that we were created as persons, male and female. In the biblical view the role of the body in imaging God is rooted in the idea that the body and soul together make the one person. They cannot be split up. In our biology lies the nuptial significance of the body and the call to communion which is fulfilled in marriage. The body is not a machine or an appendage, but our way of being in the world, in a body, incarnated. The body plays an important part in the way we image God to one another.

Feminine Qualities

Because of God's design, women have three unique qualities that, if denied, will affect the future of our society and its children. Women are life-givers; they have a capacity for concern for the person that is unique; and they have a capacity for the spiritual life. Women are uniquely made to be life-givers and to give special attention to the human person.[5] Women are the source of society, albeit not alone. They are in their persons the nurturing place for new life. The Pope writes in *The Gospel of Life*, "Motherhood involves a special communion with the mystery of life, as it develops in the woman's womb. . . . This unique contact with the new human being developing within her gives rise to an attitude towards human beings, not only towards her own child, but every human being, which profoundly marks the woman's personality."[6] The specific quality of being open and accepting of other persons is in a woman's heart and is the essence of human dignity, to be accepted because you are a person, not from other pragmatic considerations such as "usefulness, strength, intelligence, beauty or health."[7] This basic reality is the essential prerequisite for cultural change and is a gift of women to society. The gift for nurturing when directed outward is virtue and life-affirming; when directed toward self, it is selfish and destructive of what is truly feminine. Without the development of the truly feminine dimension of family life and social life, civilized human life disintegrates.

With the recognition of the unique qualities of women, men's complimentary role is clear and becomes defined in relation to her.

The third and, in the long run, the most important role for women is developing her spiritual capacity. That capacity of openness to others and to God is at the heart of the Christian religion and of what we mean by the moral life. Mary, the Mother of God, is the model of the fullest response of a creature to God because she lived this openness so well. She was a strong woman who was full of grace. She was virgin, mother, and spouse. She taught Jesus the meaning of self-sacrifice in human life while He taught her the eternal meaning of acts of love done in union with Him. Everything she did was full of grace, and this fullness of grace made the difference as she walked with Christ and with the Apostles. The most important thing a woman can do is to grow in virtue, and use her gifts for others, and develop her spiritual gifts. Woman's life-giving role should not be merely confined to external aspects of life, creating a nurturing environment, important as that is for human growth and development. We, through attention to growth in spiritual life, can touch the spiritual life of people, as well as their social-cultural life by making room for God. Ultimately this can be a leaven that can affect and change the political climate.

Openness to God

The Christian woman whose life is rooted in God is able to fulfill her unique vocation to live in openness to God and others. As she grows in virtue, she knows real spiritual freedom. Attention to individual persons matures and influences every aspect of her life, whether in the family or in professional life. Blessed Edith Stein wrote that a woman's vocation should merge with her particular vocation "and impress the latter with a feminine character." "Instead of simply functioning as a lawyer, doctor, teacher or civil servant, a woman would always have the opportunity and the obligation to serve as a motherly companion for those with whom she worked. She would never be satisfied with applying a limited technical expertise; her actions would be the outflow of her own unselfish love."[8] By this motherly quality she meant a woman's unique quality of warmheartedness and dependability that moves beyond "a little circle of family and friends."[9] In order to maintain this spirit and deepen it, a woman needs time for prayer and interior silence so that her heart can be transformed by grace. "Mary pondered all these things in her heart." Taking time for days of recollection, retreats, and down time should not be a luxury but an important part of life.

Developing her capacity for spiritual life will anchor her unique feminine gifts so needed by the Christian community. In living our openness to God we are tempted by one hundred and one distractions and potential other choices. We cannot lose our focus because that capacity of openness to God is the key to sustaining a sense of peace in our society. In his message for the World Day of Peace, Pope John Paul II directed his remarks to women. He affirmed that for women to be "teachers of peace" they must nurture peace within themselves. Peaceful women need to show special concern for other women who have suffered injustice and exploitation, those who need support, mothers raising families, single women, through groups, associations, and movements. He said, "When women are able fully to share their gifts with the whole community, the very way in which society understands and organizes itself is improved and comes to reflect in a better way the substantial unity of the human family."[10] There can be no real peace without the unique feminine presence in the family and in society. I think of this when I hear children say that they never sit down to a dinner with the whole family. That situation often comes back to the woman's choices and priorities.

A Culture of Life

Spiritually strengthened, we can pursue the work of building a culture of life. It is a culture that welcomes human life and supports it in a loving environment; a culture that reflects on authentic womanhood and defends a biblical view of the complementarity of men and women; a culture that is spiritually alive in Christ.

Catholic women need to be more active in order to help our society from going off the track. Catholic women have the experience and wisdom to speak about women's role in the family and in the community. We need to demonstrate to the feminists that we deeply understand the needs and gifts of women. We can reach out to those who have been wounded. Behind the flurry of feminist activism are many women who are hurting and looking for more recognition as human beings. Many lesbians are women who were abused in their youth. We have to be more actively pro-woman in the sense of seeking her greatest good, not letting her be seduced by false choices. We can, through feminine ingenuity, find many ways to stand with all persons in need at home, in the Church, in our schools, and in government. Perhaps in the end it is the unique gifts of Catholic women reaching out that may help allay some of the feminist anger and restore real peace.

Endnotes
1. *Evangelium Vitae*, n. 28.
2. *Evangelium Vitae*, n. 12.

3. U.N. PrepCom Meeting, New York, April 3, 1995.
4. John Paul II, Letter to Families, n. 40.
5. *Evangelium Vitae*, n. 99.
6. *Ibid.*
7. *Ibid.*
8. Waltraud Herbstrith, *Edith Stein: A Biography*, p. 53.
9. *Op. cit.*, p. 54.
10. Pope's Message for World Day of Peace, *Origins*, December, 1994.

What Cradle Catholics Take for Granted

Our Holy Father, John Paul II, has called us to participate in the new evangelization of the Catholic Church. I offer you these very personal remarks about my experience as a convert in the Catholic Church in hopes that you can use them to engage people around you, friends and family, who have lost heart in their faith — who have given up. Perhaps through my eyes, through my words, you can see ways of reaching out to them once again, and help bring them home.

It's only human nature for us to take things for granted: family, country, religion. But there's a special problem among Catholics about taking their faith for granted. I didn't know this when I entered the Church over a decade ago. I found out about it in the course of answering the many questions that came my way about my conversion.

I was constantly asked, how would a Southern Baptist minister from Fort Worth, Texas, make his way to Rome? As I would share my story, enthusiastically as any ex-Baptist must, I found that enthusiasm doesn't get you very far among Catholics. I was met with blank stares.

I started classifying those blank stares. The first classification was, "What is he talking about? Aquinas, Natural Law, Maritain. I've never heard of that!" The other set of blank stares I classified as, "I thought we'd done away with this kind of Catholicism."

Discovery of Catholic Tradition

So, as I moved through the first decade of my life as a Catholic, I began to realize that some Catholics did, in fact, take their Church and its great legacy for granted. If you'd ask me, "What do we cradle Catholics take for granted?" I would say Catholic wisdom, Catholic doctrine, and the Mass.

I used to look forward to questions on my conversion until I started meeting incredulity and hostility. I loved to tell the story about my discovery of Catholic wisdom at Princeton Theological Seminary, one of the greatest Protestant seminaries in this country, through the great work of St. Augustine, *On the Trinity*. As I read *On the Trinity*, I encountered something I had never seen in any of the great Protestant theologians I had read: the perfect cooperation of natural and supernatural intelligence. A command of history. A command of classical learning. The invention of the psychological method.

This encounter with St. Augustine led me to more years of reading than I care to admit. I'm embarrassed it took me so long after that to enter the Church. I should have known better. I read Aquinas. I read the Church Fathers. I read the great Reformation and Post-Reformation debates. I read the great Catholic novelists, whom I still recommend to you. I read the great Catholic poets. I listened to your music. I tried to learn your language. *Have you tried to learn your language?*

This culminated in a reading of the two volumes of the documents of Vatican II. I read those documents because I had read a book by James Hitchcock called *Decline and Fall: Catholicism and Modernity* which made me worry that the Church I so yearned to enter was becoming Protestant. When I finished those documents of Vatican II, I realized very clearly that the Church that I had first glimpsed in the life and work of St. Monica's son still existed. It hadn't changed.

When I went to my first Mass and tried to get a grip on all of that movement, all of that unexpected motion, all of those inconsecutive page numbers, it was a lot harder and it took a lot longer to assimilate. But finally, it dawned on me that just as there is tremendous power in your wisdom and in your doctrine, the greatest power of all is in your Eucharist. Your worship culminates an encounter with the objective presence of Christ on the altar.

Perhaps you hear this Baptist enthusiasm welling up in me, but I'll try to hold it down. I know that enthusiastic stories of converts are met with a little bit of suspicion. Ronald Knox, bless his soul, wrote this great book called *Enthusiasm: A Chapter in the History of Religion.* I sometimes wish it had never been written. Every time I mention to my Catholic friends, one exception being Mother Angelica, who agrees with me on this, that we need a little more enthusiasm in the Catholic Church, I hear "Oh, Ronald Knox, Ronald Knox." I don't think he meant to expunge all of the fun out of our faith. I think we know the kind of dangers he was warning us against.

Most Catholics, I think, are baffled why anyone would choose to carry the baggage of this old outdated faith. I'm here as living proof that this is not a religion only acquired by birth. In fact, if you think back through Church history, isn't it true that large families alone didn't make the Catholic Church great. Large families alone didn't make the Catholic Church endure. It was evangelization that made the Catholic Church great. Evangelization made it the universal Church — global in its scope.

The Church grew because missionaries shared the faith, told the stories. We can't just rely on having large families to keep the Catholic Church great. Large families are wonderful. They're a blessing. What will keep the Catholic Church great is a commitment to telling the stories, to evangelization, to witnessing. When is the last time you did it? When is the last time you were able to articulate to your alienated Catholic friends why you remain a Catholic?

We all take things for granted. We take our families for granted. We take our country for granted. We take our religion for granted. But in this case of family and country, I've noticed there's kind of an automatic correction that goes on. You get older, you have children, and you think, "My mother and father, how great they were. How grateful I am to them. Why didn't I realize it until now?" It happens kind of automatically, at least it did for me. This

---

last Veteran's Day hit me the hardest of any Veteran's Day that I've ever known. For some reason I thought about thousands of people who have died so that I could be free, so that I could raise my daughter in a free country. I'm sure as I grow older, this love of country will just get stronger and stronger.

The Mind of Christ

But there's a special problem with the Catholic Church. There's no evidence that cradle Catholics who fall away, who lose heart, there is no evidence they return. When I ask them why they haven't returned, they are inarticulate. They don't really know why. They use phrases about the irrelevancy of an authoritarian masculine church, about the lack of women priests, about nuns who were mean to them in the third grade. But in all of this they've not taken on the mind of Christ. They've taken on the mind of the media. The mind of Christ was never imparted to them.

We have to take this indifference seriously, because the fate of our children is at stake. We now live in an era we call "modernity." Modernity is defined by options — an almost unlimited range of options for young people. Our young people are not automatically going to choose the faith of their parents. Protestant evangelicals are wooing them. The culture at large is wooing them — the secular culture — and they have very powerful tools on their side. They have the movies on their side. They have films on their side.

Why would your children, when they come to an age of decision, and of course ages of decision rise all through life — why would they want to return to a lukewarm, lethargic, inarticulate Church? Why? When there's so much passionate commitment elsewhere. Don't tell me the Catholic Church should be a place where enthusiasm is excluded. That's nonsense. We should be just as excited about the gifts we have in our Church than any other gifts, than any other pleasures.

Another sign of a special problem in the Catholic Church is

what I call the "post-office phenomenon." People who can't explain what they are doing hide behind a posture. People who think they alone deliver the spiritual mail but can't explain *why*, will make you stand in line until they're ready to serve you — but don't ask any questions in the meantime! How can the Church expect people to remain faithful, devoted, and grateful when they're being treated like that?

Catholic faith is old, yes. It is venerable, yes. But it still needs to be explained to each new generation, your children and their children. May I remind you that the older generation needs a refresher course from time to time? That's why you're reading *Crisis* magazine and other Catholic publications.

Wisdom, doctrine, and worship — the very reasons I became a Catholic — are being taken for granted.

Catholic Liberation

What does it mean for me to discover your Church? First, it was totally liberating for a Baptist to realize that Christian intelligence is not limited merely to citing text from Scripture to support arguments, but rather that Christian intelligence takes in the whole of the natural order, and that God speaks through the natural order to the prudent eye. This was nothing less than the recovery of my intellect, the intellect that God gave me to use.

Second, it was liberating to realize that the biblical revelation, the revelation through the prophets, through Christ, had been contained, reflected and commented upon throughout the history of the Church, which is the body of Christ. That a weighing and sifting had gone on for all of these centuries gave me the confidence that I didn't have to jump back 1,800 or 1,900 years every time I wanted to know what Christ calls me to do. This, for me, was nothing less than a recovery of human history.

For a Baptist to come into the Catholic Mass, to realize that the culmination of worship does not come in response to a man's voice, however melodious, however articulate, but comes in response to the objective actual presence of Christ, was nothing less than a recovery of the full meaning of the Incarnation.

I maintain that all human beings, not just Baptists, hunger for this kind of liberation. For the recovery of the whole person and all of human history. Notice there's nothing extraneous about these issues. These are not intellectual issues. These are not academic issues. These are the very issues that distinguish us as Catholics, not Protestants; Catholics, not Jews; Catholics, not secularists. It's what makes us Catholic.

These are the very issues — wisdom, doctrine, and worship — that give us our advantage in the public square. Ralph Reed of the Christian Coalition welcomed Catholics to the public square. It's sad that we haven't been there when we have much more ammunition to bring than anybody else. Pope John Paul II's speech on human rights at the United Nations is a paradigm to which we should all aspire.

The Catholic Advantage

For the last ten years, I took on a research project on the meaning of human happiness. It was a project inspired by my entry into the Catholic Church. I bring this up as an example of what I mean by the Catholic advantage in the public square — in politics, in the arts, in the humanities, in the social sciences. If we look at the way the meaning of human happiness has been misrepresented and made superficial in the twentieth century — the way it has affected our political life, our moral life, our family life, and our education — we realize that the corrective is to go back to the Tradition. Back to Catholic wisdom. Back to the Bible. Back to Augustine and Aquinas. To Jacques Maritain and Christopher Dawson, Martin D'Arcy, and G. K. Chesterton. We must go back. What we will find there is a way to correct our problem. There is a wisdom there. There are ideas there that can have consequences for us. We can change things not just by adjusting public policy but by fixing ideas that we live by.

How can you take for granted a legacy which has everything we need to know about telling the story of the good life? Not just the good life in private, at home, but the good life lived publicly. The good life in the world of work. The good life in the world of the arts. The good life in the academic world. It is not a story to be divided between public and private. It is a story to be brought to bear on the whole of civilization. It *has been* brought to bear on the whole of civilization. The books in my library are rows deep. They're all there: Dawson, Maritain, Chesterton, Murray, Neuhaus, Novak, Weigel. I'm perplexed by Catholics that know nothing about the amazing influence, the formative benefit of the Catholic Church on world civilization.

Certainly you know about the role of the Catholic Church in the formation of hospitals, universities, libraries, social services of all kinds, the growth of economics, the development of democracy, the emergence of freedom. The next time someone trying to intimidate you brings up the inquisition, don't resort to some sort of misplaced notion of charity or tolerance and apologize for your Church. Say, "Oh, sure, we've made mistakes but what about universities, hospitals, and democratic institutions, the notion of the human person itself, which arose right out of the heart of the Church — nowhere else?"

Wisdom

When the historian Arthur Schlesinger talks about the self-correcting aspects of Western civilization and its superiority, he could have well said that Catholic wisdom had a great deal to do with the self-correcting dimension of Western civilization.

Catholic wisdom particularly protects the family. Catholic wisdom, which takes in both divine revelation and reflection on the world of nature, testifies to the ordinate union of men and women in marriage, not random arrangements. These ordinate unions are the ones that should be protected and nurtured by law.

Consider the situation now in the state of Hawaii. What we

need to realize — those of us committed to public Catholicism — is that the problem there is not just same-sex marriage. The problem there, which is growing among Catholics in Hawaii, is that many issues are coalescing into one horrible stew which is about to boil over. Same-sex marriage, allied with the gay rights movement, with multiculturalism, with national sovereignty, with new-age liturgy and spirituality, is making it very difficult for our brothers and sisters in Hawaii.

Public Catholicism of the type the Catholic Campaign for America is espousing requires us to be well armed with wisdom and doctrine. We're going to start with the writings of our Pope. We're going to read his books, we're going to read his encyclicals, we're going to read his speeches.

Converts go through a kind of Catholic retooling process. That's why some of us have a fairly explicit, if not always entirely accurate, grasp of its principles. I asked my wife, who is also a Baptist convert from the south, if her meeting me had anything to do with her becoming Catholic. She said, "Yes, meeting you and your circle of friends in Atlanta. . . . The one thing that kept coming through as I listened to your discussions is the fundamental notion that life is good: Life is good regardless of the pain of that life, regardless of the suffering, regardless of the obstacles to be overcome, regardless of what is missing materially from that life, regardless of the fact that a life may not be loved by some human being that should love it."

That life is good is one of the first principles of Catholic wisdom. It is the principle we invoke to save our unborn children. It is the principle we invoke when we explain our position on birth control to skeptics. It's the position we invoke when we discuss euthanasia. Life is good.

Doctrine

You might be thinking now, "I can't accuse my friends of taking things for granted that they never knew about." In that case, it's partially the responsibility of those people who formed you in your faith — that they didn't pass it on. We all know there's been a great confusion about Catholic doctrine in the last forty years, but what do we have now that we didn't have two years ago? We have the *Catechism of the Catholic Church.*

Your amateur experts in your parish and your Catholic schools can't invent theology on the spot anymore because you can look in the *Catechism* yourself. You read the section on the sacraments. They are not psychologized; sacraments don't exist to make you feel good. In fact, they exist to make you feel bad sometimes. That can be good for you, that can lead you to happiness, that can be part of your happiness. The sacraments in the *Catechism* aren't politicized, aren't communalized. They are the power of God sustaining us from birth, conception to eternity — not to death — *through* death to eternity. They are the participation in the life of God that can only be lost by outright rejection — not by sin, not by failings, not by death.

In my journey through the Church, one of my most important moments was a passage that I read in a book by Hans Urs von Balthasar, *The Heart of the World.* It read something like this: "Because of Christ and His sacraments, none of us can fall so low that we don't fall into the arms of God." It was a very powerful message for me then and it still is.

Worship

This brings me to my last point. Worship. What can be done to revitalize it so it can't be taken for granted? It's a more difficult question because we just can't hand people a book like the *Catechism*; we can't just ask people to read John Paul II's *Documents on Liturgy and Worship* because worship is something that is done in a particular place, at a particular time, among particular people. Books aren't enough. Something else has to happen.

I have a hunch what that is. I don't have any survey data to support me on this, but I've noticed that whenever there is vital worship, there are people who pray. The common denominator that I have seen between a vital worship, something that works, something that draws me in, is that people are at prayer. It is the power of prayer at work through the celebrant, the power of prayer at work through the people that is transformative. It's a transformation that is immediately intuited by everyone present.

This reminded me of a great lesson I was taught by Jacques and Raïssa Maritain. In one of the first books they ever wrote — they wrote it together in the 1920's, *Prayer and Intelligence* — they argue, indeed they celebrate, that prayer, intelligence, and worship reach toward the same source. That each act is bathed in the same iridescent and illuminating light — a divine light.

I hope by now you realize that I'm not saying that cradle Catholics are at a disadvantage. After all, my wife and I have made a long journey; a long journey to have an opportunity to lay a Catholic in our cradle. It's not easy to enter this Church. You don't make it easy. And you shouldn't. I thank God that our seven-year-old daughter, Hannah Clare Hudson, is a cradle Catholic. I make you these promises, these promises in gratitude for your Church that has received us, the Church of your forebears. I promise you that I will share with her, my daughter, all the wisdom I've learned. I promise you that I will do my best, with the help of our wonderful parish school, to make sure she understands the glories of Catholic teaching. I promise you I will pray with her each and every day and at Mass. And most of all I promise that I will pray to God that neither Hannah Clare, nor her parents will ever take the gift of His Church for granted.

A Catholic Perspective to the Cultural War

We are called day by day to the duty of choosing between the Culture of Life and the Culture of Death. The Holy Father, in *Evangelium Vitae*, writes about a particularly pressing need at the present time, when the Culture of Death so forcefully opposes the Culture of Life, and often seems to have the upper hand. I have taken these words myself as a kind of a guiding light in terms of a number of issues that I have tried to address in the past, and will continue to address in the future.

Popular Music

I believe that American society right now is perilously caught up with the Culture of Death in a number of ways and in a number of contexts. Let me address one that is of particular interest to me. It started about a year ago when DeLores Tucker (she is head of the National Political Congress of Black Women, and is a liberal Democrat) and I went after Interscope Records, a Time Warner-owned company which produced vulgar, offensive rap music. Why were we so agitated about this? The following lyrics will show you why I think this kind of music qualifies as the Culture of Death, of which the Pope speaks. One of the songs produced at one time by Time Warner, was by a group called the "Geto Boys":

> Her body is beautiful, so I'm thinking rape
> Grab the bitch by the mouth, drug her back in
> Slam her down on the couch, whipped out my knife
> And said if you scream, I'm cuttin'
> She begged in a low voice, please don't kill me
> I slit her throat and watched her shake, like on TV.

That's music. That's entertainment. That's the kind of stuff that we read to the Chairman of the Board, the President, and others at Time Warner, and asked them how it is that they justified selling that to children for profit in a free society. Did they see anything wrong with that? We then asked them whether there was anything so gross, so horrible, or so vulgar that they wouldn't sell it. And in the pause that followed, in the silence that followed, I thought I heard a civilization and a culture slipping away.

Well, Time Warner paid some attention to it. They made the right decision. They got rid of this company. The music still exists, but at least for now, it's out of one part of American life. At least for now, it's out of the mainstream. At least for now, it's not being produced and distributed by one of America's major companies. Now other companies may purchase Interscope, and if they do, we will address this issue again. But for now, it's in the back alley, and although it doesn't belong anywhere, it is better in the back alley than on the thoroughfare.

If that's not the Culture of Death, I don't know what is.

Television

Similarly, a couple of weeks ago, Senator Joseph Lieberman, an orthodox Jew, and I had a press conference during which we talked about a number of television talk shows. While we were having breakfast, talking about our press conference that was going to follow, we got a call from Senator Sam Nunn. Senator Nunn asked if he could join us at the press conference, saying that he didn't think anything that was going on in the Senate that day was as important as talking about the content of these shows. So we welcomed Senator Nunn at the press conference.

We said that we didn't think that the achievement of indecent exposure necessitated putting it on television and celebrating it as a virtue. We said that as men of faith, different faiths, but of faith, that we understood the need for human beings to confess. We understood the need for human beings to talk about their faults and their failures, and that in the traditions out of which we each come, that was often done by talking to an all-knowing and an all-forgiving God — a God from whom no secrets are hidden, from whom no hearts are closed. We understood the need of human beings for confession and disclosure. We discussed how, in the past, personal failure or marital failure was often an occasion for personal reflection, for confession and prayer with the God from whom no secrets are hidden. We acknowledged that we have come a long way, a long way down, when personal failure is now not an occasion for such reflection — for thoughtfulness and for prayer — but is rather a ticket to appear on the *Sally Jessy Raphael* show, where one can talk about how everything went wrong in one's personal life and relationship before a studio audience and a television audience of millions.

If this isn't the culture of disintegration; if this isn't the culture of decomposition; if this isn't the Culture of Death, I don't know what is. Senator Lieberman and I said in our statement at that press conference that it's because we are men who believe in God and believe that human beings are moral and spiritual creatures that we find these shows so unpleasant, so unsatisfying, so degrading, so degenerate, and so unworthy of anyone's support. In his "Letter from Birmingham City Jail," Martin Luther King wrote that "What degrades human nature is unjust. What uplifts human nature is just." If these shows do not degrade human nature, I don't know what does.

Abortion

But there can be no conversation about the Culture of Life and the Culture of Death without talking about our public policies, our laws, and the situation in the United States when it comes to the topic of abortion. As a Catholic and a member of the board for the Catholic Campaign for America, I feel I must address — many of us must address — without hesitation, and with the proper degree of moral seriousness, this issue of abortion in America. One and a half million abortions are performed every year, of which the overwhelming majority are performed on perfectly healthy children. This number is a national shame and a national catastrophe. But not only is this catastrophic itself, it is also horrible in its other consequences on the sensibilities of the American people.

I think there can be little doubt that the thirty million abortions since 1973 have had a coarsening effect on a people's attitude toward its children. It has diminished our sense of responsibility, the obligation imposed on each generation of adults by the next generation of children to come, and indeed, it has accelerated the growth of what Pope John Paul II has correctly called the Culture of Death.

In addressing this issue, we should never abandon principle. We should invite as many people as possible to the affirmation of our clear and unambiguous position, and to our efforts to reduce significantly the number of abortions in this country. But I do believe that reasonable people of good will can and do disagree on the means to that end. Some would push for various forms of criminalization, for example. Some would not. Some believe the constitutional amendment outlining abortion is the surest and best way to get there. Others, in good faith, doubt this. Differences aside, it seems to me that we ought to bring to the cause all those who look at the figure of 1.5 million abortions a year with horror and misgivings. They should all be our allies. We could admit that there may be some hard, some wrenching cases on which some people of good will can disagree. But let's set aside the small number of hard cases and focus our efforts on the vast majority of cases where most Americans of all faiths do not feel ambiguity at all.

My own view is this: I believe *Roe* v. *Wade* was wrongly decided and based on flawed legal reasoning. Second, I support legislative efforts to expand the boundaries of legal protection for the unborn, such as waiting periods, parental notification, restrictions of abortions after viability, and other such measures. On these restrictions, of course, Bob Casey is the man whose example all governors should follow. I oppose the use of public funds to pay for abortion, and I strongly support pro-life alternatives such as adoption and abstinence. As for the specific issue of the constitutional amendment, I know many people feel strongly about it. For myself, I do not think it will do much good and I also believe there may well be drawbacks to it. Above all, I believe it will do nothing to help reduce the number of abortions, and this is, after all, the crucial issue in this debate.

How do we reduce the number of abortions in America? Abortion is a moral issue, and the law should reflect that fact. Current law refuses to demonstrate to people that abortion is even a serious issue, much less a moral one. Our efforts should be to infuse into the law a heightened sense of the human and the spiritual dimensions of the issue: provisions which highlight and stress the morality of the issue, waiting periods, information about fetal life, possible consequences for the mother, parental notification, etc. These should be pursued vigorously and can be often successfully pursued at the state level. I believe that there is a pro-life agenda that is both incremental and principled, both politically realistic and ambitious.

Politically Realistic

Our nation as it is today will sustain certain legal reforms. It will sustain ending late-term abortions and sex-selection abortions. It will sustain promoting informed consent, and it will sustain requiring parental notification to end the desperate isolation of pregnant teenagers and to promote responsibility, communication, and mature decision-making. That is where we ought to concentrate our legal efforts. Those are the places where we should put our legal energies. I recognize that some pro-life groups will consider this kind of incremental effort as too little. To which I respond, the approach I'm advocating recognizes that social reform must respect political realities if we hope to restrict abortion on demand, if we hope to get the numbers down. Public sentiment is everything. Lincoln once said of American democracy, "With public sentiment, nothing can fail; without it, nothing can succeed. Consequently, he who molds public sentiment, goes deeper than he who enacts statutes or pronounces decisions. He makes statutes and decisions possible or impossible to be executed." So let us move public opinion so that statutes and laws can be changed. I believe this type of pro-life movement would find the support of the majority of Americans, including many Democrats who are deeply troubled by the massive number of abortions which take place every year.

There is an instructive historical analogy to which we can turn. Research by Marvin Olasky, the author of *Abortion Rites: A Social History of Abortion in America*, has revealed something that many Americans on both sides of the abortion debate do not know. At the outset of the Civil War, the abortion rate in a smaller U.S. population was almost exactly what it is today. A pro-life movement based on a network of shelters began to actively oppose abortion by providing refuge to women in trouble. Institutions like the YWCA, the Salvation Army, and Florence Crittingdon Homes concentrated their efforts among prostitutes and young urban women who were impregnated and then abandoned. These activists worked for small victories; they provided women with positive pro-life alternatives to abortion; and they fought for laws while not making them their primary focus. The result? Between 1860 and 1910, steady and compassionate social pressure reduced the rate of abortions by over one-half, and the rate stayed low until about 1960, when what I call the great havoc began. This model, what Olasky referred to as containment as a way to achieve rollback, is precisely the model anti-abortion advocates should look to and learn from. I believe it is politically viable and ultimately more effective and life-affirming.

In another historical analogy, some might have compared abortion in this century with slavery a century and a half ago. Many indeed have been coming to this view lately. Many defenders of the rights of Blacks have different views on which specific efforts to abolish slavery in a democratic republic would have proven most expedient, prudent, and fruitful. There were passionate debates about an important issue, and indeed, there should have been. I believe the course of action chosen by abolitionists like Harriet Tubman offer greater promise than the course chosen by John Brown. Again, I think we could learn much from Lincoln, who proposed containing slavery so as to put it on the path to extinction. The spirit of both Harriet Tubman and Abraham Lincoln would well serve the pro-life movement today.

Finally, I want to express my deep respect for the pro-life people who labor long and hard and selflessly on behalf of the unborn. I speak here of people you know: the people in the crisis pregnancy centers, in the adoption agencies, and in the foster homes around this country. The work is among the most important and admirable in the nation. These are the people who are doing the most to contain and to reduce the number of abortions in America, and they are doing it one at a time. They are the unsung heroes of our republic. It's time to give them the praise they deserve.

Our major cultural task, indeed I think our major task over all, is the redirection of this Culture of Death. It has been put for us quite squarely and quite eloquently by the Holy Father himself: It is our challenge.

Interior Renewal and Public Action

In good Trinitarian fashion, I'd like to discuss the interior life, interior renewal, and public action.

First, these two important aspects of our lives, the interior and public, are not the same. Sometimes there are very good people with a strong interior life who are, in the public world, naive, not very skillful, and quite easily manipulated by people who are evil or perhaps only out for their own self-interest. There are many cases in history of good people who failed in the public sphere quite colossally. On the other hand, sometimes one encounters in history or even in life, people who are not very good personally, who do not have a very profound interior life, who are rather shallow, but who nonetheless have rare public talents, and have rare insight into how things work. Sometimes they even know how to make things better for their people and for their nation.

Now, it's three times more difficult to have a holy inner life than just to have an ordinary life. And it's three times more difficult to be good, really good in public life, than merely to be a more or less passive citizen. But to put both of them together is not the addition of 3 + 3; it's 3 squared, 9 times more difficult! It's not difficulty added; it's squared. Nonetheless, that is the Catholic and Christian ideal: to keep both of those projects united.

The Divine Image

The image we have been given for this balance of the inner and the outer life is the incarnation of God Himself, who took all the glory of divinity and enfleshed it in the humility of one man, born of one woman, in one place — a very poor place, not the grandest of places, but a very humble place — and who, because He was flesh, did not immediately reveal to people or show to people that He was God.

We sometimes think it would be lovely to live in the time of Christ and to have seen Him. But in honesty, we must ask ourselves, would we have recognized Him? Would we have been among those who expected something more, something more ideal, something more utopian, in the actual appearance of God in history, than in the humble carpenter that people actually saw?

In 1995, we celebrated the thirtieth anniversary of the document on the Church in the Modern World. In November of that year, in the Vatican, the Pope appeared before an audience of about three hundred, including the Cardinals and many of those in the ministries of the laity to express his personal pleasure with *Gaudium et Spes*, "Joy and Hope" — *The Church in the Modern World*. He had been on the subcommission; he had had a significant role in proposing early in the Council that the Council focus on two things: the human person, the acting person, the subject of his great philosophical book, *The Acting Person*; and second, the community — the *communio* — of all human beings. We each have our dignity, each alone, but even more as participants in the community, which shares the life of God. The Holy Father felt privileged to have served on the commissions that finally approved this document.

A little later, up at the House of Loreto, where a conference continued for two days on this celebration, Father Joseph Tischner, one of the great philosopher priests of Poland, described how crucial *Gaudium et Spes* was for the people of Poland living under communism. From it they received reinforcement for the idea that part of their vocation as Catholics is to change the world, in addition to living a profound interior life. You could live a life committed to honesty and with fidelity to the light under communism, you could do that in prison, you could do that in the concentration camps. But Catholics are called to more than that. They are called to an engagement with the world around them.

Without *Gaudium et Spes*, Father Tischner said, there would have been no Solidarity, there would not have been those meetings in church basements of workers and intellectuals. The rebuilding in those church basements — the only free places in Poland, as many atheists have testified, ecumenical places in which people of all faiths could gather — was a rebuilding of civil society as an alternative to the state.

Human social life is not conducted for the most part through the state, it is conducted through free associations of citizens. Self-government is a capacity of citizens to govern themselves, through their own associations — associations like the Catholic Campaign — trying to fill a gap in the vitality of American society, invented and created out of the imagination of a few, but speaking to the needs of a great many.

This was happening in Poland as well. Without the reopening of civil society, without the beginning of Solidarity, the independent trade union, with a certain real power over the economy, how could anyone have imagined, Father Tischner asked, how could the collapse of communism have occurred? In short, the world which we inherited in 1995, he argued, is a direct fruit of *Gaudium et Spes*.

The Eternal Now

What was the message of *Gaudium et Spes*? That God should not be imagined as having been *before* the world, and then creating the world, and then redeeming the world, and then deciding to call into being a Church. In God it doesn't happen in steps like that. It happens all at once — an eternal now. Sometimes we have the experience of that eternal now. I loved sports when I was young — football, basketball — and it often happened that I would hear my mother calling for me across the field that dinner was ready, and it seemed like we had just started! There was no sense of time. It was as if we had lived the moment of eternity in fantastic activity, but all simultaneously in one moment. To be brought back to the world of time and schedules was a shock.

We have many such anticipations of eternity in moments of great and intense concentration of our energies — in the arts, in love, in the presence of a granddaughter.

The point is that God knew from the beginning in creating human beings that He would create human beings in and with and through His Son. In a quite powerful and immediate way, the image of what a human being ought to be, the goal, the model for a human being, was embodied in the Logos, embodied in the incarnate Jesus Christ. The technical and theological way for putting this is that Christology, the study of Christ, reveals most profoundly the depths of anthropology. Anthropology is not complete until it takes on board the possibilities that Jesus Christ revealed about the purpose, the nature, the destiny of human beings.

But there is a danger that the theologians will take over *Gaudium et Spes* by making it a part of systematic theology, with a new view of Christology and a new view of the Trinity. That's all well and good. But remember that among the Council Fathers *Gaudium et Spes* was primarily motivated by a sense that over the last two or three centuries, the Church had been too disengaged from the modern world. The Church empowered lay people too little to take their rightful places in the modern world — to suffuse it as yeast suffuses dough, and make their influence felt in every part of it, so that all of society might come to bear the gracious imprint of what God intended for it. This must be done by lay people. They are, as it were, the capillaries, the blood vessels, that carry grace to the surface of the skin of human society.

So *Gaudium et Spes* called us to be public Catholics, to be active in the world. It particularly called lay people since that's what we were made for. That's why we have been baptized. To fail in our public mission is to fail in half the purpose of our Incarnation, so to speak. We weren't incarnated, we weren't given flesh, we weren't made part of a social body, solely in order to live private lives, but also to live public lives. Indirectly, *Gaudium et Spes* warns us that this requires a different sort of interior life. Public life is very painful. People around you do not always have an interest in telling the truth about you. They do not see you the way you see yourself. Things will be said about you, if you are active at all, that are painful and will give you cause to doubt and to hesitate. There is good evidence to believe that many, many people avoid public life today because public life is so combative. There are also many people who, realizing that fact, are willing to practice intimidation. The minute you deviate from what is acceptable in public discourse, they are likely to set up demonstrations on your lawn, or to say things about you in the press designed to make you stop, or to exclude you from society and from acceptable discourse. Many people do not have thick enough skins to endure that. But those who are going to heed their own vocation to public Catholicism, to public Christianity, and even to public citizenship, are bound to feel that.

Now there's a second and entirely understandable reason why this happens. When you go to make decisions in public life for a whole community, it's not always clear what you ought to do. Take welfare reform. No one can deny, especially those of us who supported welfare reform in the 1960's, that what we now have is not what we intended. Thirty years after we declared war on poverty, we have a 600% increase in violent crime and a 500% increase in children born out of wedlock. That wasn't promised, because it wasn't foreseen, and it surely wasn't intended. Our Bishops recently warned against the devastation that might come from welfare reform, but what about the devastation we have without reform, the devastation we experience with the status quo?

Two principles were mentioned in *Gaudium et Spes* about this very fact of welfare. *Gaudium et Spes* called attention to the success of welfare programs since World War II. These gave a softer and more compassionate edge to the free society, and had already proven by 1965 to ease the suffering of Europe. In those days, the focus of Catholic social thought was mainly on Europe. Then, at

Vatican II, the world saw Bishops from all over the world in St. Peter's Basilica, and those from outside Europe were the majority for the first time ever.

Subsidiarity

Two points were made about welfare in *Gaudium et Spes*: One is the principle of subsidiarity: the right way to order society is to have decisions made as close to the people as possible, and made at farther away levels only when necessary. Consider the welfare rolls in New Hampshire and in Massachusetts. AFDC caseload in New Hampshire is about 27,000. In neighboring Massachusetts it is 265,000. In New Hampshire, it may be possible to organize the churches so that in effect each church could take responsibility for one such family. Businesses could be reorganized to help find jobs for so relatively few people. But in Massachusetts with a far heavier caseload, no informal set of organizations is likely to be as successful.

Doesn't it make a certain sense, then, to return the decisions about welfare to the states, so that each of the 50 states, considering their own particular vulnerability and needs, could design these programs to fit their circumstances more closely, rather than have all these decisions made at one federal level, the same for all? That would seem the working out of the Catholic principle of subsidiarity. (Incidentally, the first quote giving the essence of the principle of subsidiarity in *Sacramentum Mundi, An Encyclopedia of Theology*, is taken from Abraham Lincoln: "The legitimate object of government is to do for a community of people whatever they need to have done but cannot do at all or cannot so well do for themselves in their separate and individual capacities. In all that people can individually do as well for themselves, government ought not to interfere." American federalism is an anticipation of the principle of subsidiarity.

Human Beings Act

Second, a theme very clearly stated in *Gaudium et Spes* and in all Catholic social teaching ever since is the importance of the acting person. The dignity of the human person is that each of us, each woman and each man, is made in the image of God. Each is made in the image of Providence, to be provident over our own destiny. It is our choice whether to say yes or no to the entrance of God into our lives, and the expansion of His action into our actions. We are the ones who must say yes or no. What gives us our dignity is our capacity to say yes or no.

We have two cats at home. Peppie and LeBeau were brought home by our daughters, who promised to take care of them forever. Our daughters are gone. We can't leave home without hiring cat-sitters. I hate cats. Peppie is black and white and quick as could be and very thin. LeBeaux le duc d'Orange — if you want the full name my daughters gave him — is orange as you might guess, and is fat and slow and not clever. My wife and I don't have to worry about what career our cats are going to choose. Our children are constantly surprising us, alas. They imagine futures we never dreamt of. They act. Cats just behave. Cats don't act. They go on behaving the way cats have always behaved since the first one posed for the Sphinx. For thousands of years cats have been that way. Human beings act.

That is Wojtyla's point in his book *The Act of Reason*. Human beings imagine new futures and choose and execute them. That makes human beings a different sort of creature than cats or horses and more like God. Humans are provident for their lives and their individual human stories.

Catholic social thought has regularly warned that welfare programs, badly designed, take away from human beings their capacity for being provident over their own lives and make them totally dependent upon the state, as in a modern from of serfdom or slavery. Serfdom of the kind that Toqueville predicted would be the end of democracy in America, the new soft tyranny where all your wants are provided for, so long as you agree not to make any decisions of your own, and to live in a less than fully responsible way.

Now what should we do about this? There is indecision in the country. Almost everybody in this country believes we should end welfare as we know it, as President Clinton says. But on the other hand, if we make this reform or that reform, what will happen? We don't always know. That's the way it is with lay life, and this is the point I want to come to at the end. Lay people are always asked to make decisions about actions when we don't know what all the consequences will be.

A Fundamental Respect

Bill Doherty of the AFL-CIO is a man I greatly admire. Among the people I've met over the years, maybe no one has worked more for Catholic social thought in the active arena. He was active in Latin America for thirty-four years trying to oppose dictators, trying to build democracies, trying to strengthen free labor unions — not labor unions captured by the state, but free labor unions. He was trying to encourage and inspire the building of civil associations in which people do things for themselves, from being poll watchers at election time to organizing unions. Often he saw people that he loved and cared for killed or in danger. His wife, Jane, had five children in three different countries in the early days of their marriage.

Bill and I don't always agree in our analysis of what's going on in society, and this, too, is the situation of lay people. There are many people I deeply admire, whose sense of commitment to Catholic social teaching and to their vocation as Christians is undeniable. They shame us by comparison. And yet, as Pope John Paul II recently said, Catholic social thought is not an ideology. You don't have to sign up on a dotted line. It's not a part of a political party. It's a set of moral and religious principles, and above them all is the image of Christ. Yet prudent people trying to use their own best judgment will make different decisions.

Therefore, being a follower of Catholic social thought, being involved in Catholic public life, requires an inner life that allows you to be a little bit detached from your own opinions. Whatever you think your own vision of Catholic social thought ought to be, you need to be a little bit detached from it to recognize that there are others who have a rather different prudential understanding of what we should do here and now, which analysis we should accept, which actions we should undertake. If you don't have that detachment, it's very hard to have a society where people are civil to one another. Assume that others, too, are reasonable. Assume that each of us may have a part of the truth, even when we dramatically disagree.

One of the inspiring things about American public life in the eyes of people in Europe, Latin America, and elsewhere, is the peace after an election, how Americans accept the decision of the process, and respect it, even though they may hate one another's guts. They may disagree with one another and criticize one another. But they're also able to go out and have a cup of coffee together. It's important for us sometimes to sit down and explore a little bit why it is *you* have the silly ideas you have, and why it is you don't understand how what *I'm* saying is so wise, practical, and accurate. In a democratic society, in a society respectful of persons, you have to do that.

Thomas Aquinas once said, "Civilization is constituted by conversation." Civilized people address one another as reasonable persons and argue with them. They have a conversation. An argument addressed to one another's minds and imaginations and, of course, sentiments and passions. Civilized people argue with one another in friendliness. Barbarians club one another.

To build a civilization of love, Pope John Paul II's phrase, is above all to build a civilization in which such arguments can occur. In which Catholics from left, right, and center, indifferent, active, and everything else, can show a fundamental respect for one another, not only at the communion rail, but in our conversation. That's very difficult to maintain.

Let me show you how difficult it is to maintain: The only place in which pluralism still exists in America is at the extended family dinner at Thanksgiving. The rest of the year you go out with your friends, with people you agree with, and whose sense of humor you share. Most of the year, in other words, you go with birds of a feather. Only at Thanksgiving are you bound to sit down with family members whose views on gender drive you up the wall, whose views on economics sound to you like fingernails across a blackboard, whose views on politics fill you with such indignation, it's all you can do to stay at the table. Staying at the table year after year only happens in loving families. That's what families are for. They're not for sentimental love. They're for love that binds us to people who are so close to us that the edges of their disapproval really hurt. So we have to be realistic about family and realistic about what it is to have a Catholic community. Family isn't all sentiment. But it must be, in the end, civil. We must be able to talk out things with one another.

The Importance of the Inner Life

Let me conclude on this note. A strong inner life is necessary for the sense of detachment. This ability to be civil, even when our passions don't want to be civil, this ability to step back and gain a little distance to maintain the conversation, even when we don't want to, requires an anchor in eternity. We have to have an inner life that allows us to go on even when we've been defeated. When we've lost again and again, and we have to keep coming back because it's right. Because the cause is the right one to fight, and we weren't called to reap, but to sow. We weren't called to enjoy the victories, but to fight the fight. Especially regarding the right to life, the generation coming after us may reap the great benefits of the work we do now. They will know because by then movies will be showing what actually happened when an infant was aborted. What was the actual physical procedure with scissors and drills, and the suction that removed the brain, what dismemberment entailed? People will wonder fifty years from now how a civilized society allowed such a horror to go on a million and a half times a year.

And people will one day be proud that in those days there were voices that said it can't go on. It's wrong and we're going to persuade you by argument, with patience, in a civil way. We are going to persuade the public until, one by one, those who are in favor of abortion begin to see why they can't be in favor. They cannot defend in public what is going on. Those who say they're defending "choice," not abortion, are ducking the issue. Everybody has to choose of course, but the moral issue is always *what* you choose. Just as people today praise the abolitionists, who were regarded as troublemakers before the Civil War, so in the future they will praise those who upheld one of those rights with which our Creator has endowed us.

Of course, at the moment when we have to act, we cannot see the future. Lay people are always in a position of having to make decisions when they're not sure of the outcome. When we can't be certain that our particular practical judgment about how to proceed is going to work. So many things well intended don't work. Therefore, our model is often not the great glorious Christ, the Redeemer that we celebrate in the Liturgy, but the Christ who is rejected, who is abject, who is despised. We'll often be despised — like the suffering servant of Isaiah 53.

We may be vilified if we fight certain battles, and the way we find Christ is in being constant when we seem rejected.

Again, we often find Christ where we don't see Christ; all we see are the things that were made, the humble ordinary things of ordinary life, and yet we know all of them were made in and through Christ. Christ is that Logos in whom, and by whom, and with whom all things were made. We take nourishment from Him as Thomas Aquinas once wrote that sacramentals, as distinct from sacraments, are all those things that speak to us of God, as a glorious day speaks to us of the grace of God, and as a bad sermon comes to us like a crucifixion. "We are blest by everything;

everything we look upon is blest," William Butler Yeats wrote. And Georges Bernanos wrote in the *Diary of a Country Priest*, "Everything is grace."

That world of darkness and ambiguity is the world of lay people, and we are obliged to carry the Church into that world and to carry it with good grace, with good spirit. That requires a profound inner life. We learn by suffering that we need a much deeper inner life than we might have expected in the blush of youth. The present moment, though, is a time for the joy of battle — so much to do, so ripe a moment for action. It is a time of great grace for an organization such as this.

Catholic / Evangelical Relations

I remember when we first had Bill Bennett to the first Christian Coalition meeting about three years ago, I think he was the first major Catholic speaker that we had, and I took him around to the various seminars that were going on. A reporter came up to him and stopped him in the hall and said, "Bill, what are you doing here?" And Bill said, "I was invited." And the guy said, "But you aren't Catholic?" And he said, "Yes, I am." And Bill proceeded to get up and give a barnstorming, motivating speech as he always does and in the middle of the applause someone said, "Nail it to the door, Bill!" And he said, "Well, there goes the Catholic / Evangelical Coalition."

A Nation Renewed

I believe that the emerging alliance, the emerging partnership of Catholics and Evangelical Protestants is going to be the most powerful force in the electorate in the 1990's and beyond. I think anybody who tries to ignore that alliance is going to make a big mistake. And I want to commend you for your growing membership, for your vibrant leadership, for your public witness, and for your clear vision of a nation renewed and of a faith emboldened and reinvigorated. I believe that this organization, and the movement that it more broadly represents, stands on the threshold of a new Catholic moment in American history. The Catholic Campaign released a survey yesterday which demonstrates what most of us in this room already knew, and that is that America's 58 million Catholics, who make up about one-fourth of the electorate, are speaking out more forcefully about the social ills and the social pathologies that affect America than ever before. I will tell you something, what has happened in this country since late 1994 could not have happened had it not been for the involvement and the unprecedented support of Roman Catholics in all fifty states all across America.

A Moral Leadership

Today, at this time, we are in an extraordinary moment in the history of our nation, in our politics, and in our relationship as Protestants and as Catholics. Let there be no mistake about it that what is going on here is not a debate between Republicans and Democrats. It's not a debate between accountants. It's not about whether or not we ought to use Congressional Budget Office or Office of Management and Budget figures to determine what we're going to spend every year. It is not just a rhetorical disagreement; it is a disagreement about fundamental values that boils down to this. On one side is a group of people who believe that we ought to maintain the government and the policies that we have pursued for most of the last half century. These policies are socially permissive — the distribution of birth control in the schools without the permission of parents; the teaching of homosexuality in the public schools as an accepted alternative lifestyle; abortion-on-demand paid for with our tax dollars; making the taking of the innocent life of a baby the most common surgical procedure in America today; and fiscal and monetary profligacy, handing to our children a debt that is so out of control and so irresponsible, that children born in America today will each pay $183,000 in taxes during their lifetime just to pay their share of the interest on the national debt.

That is on one side, and then on the other side is a group of people who believe that there is a problem that ails America. It is ultimately not a fiscal problem, or a monetary problem, or a deficit problem; it is a moral problem. And I want to tell you that if they eliminated that deficit tomorrow and they do not address the moral and spiritual crisis that ails America, we will not be able to turn this country around.

On the one side are those who believe that the federal government is the answer to all of our problems, and on the other are those who believe that the failed and discredited and bureaucratic welfare state should be replaced by a society and a culture of caring and compassion. What this is really about is, who is best able among us to meet the needs and to help the hurting, the downtrodden, the poor, the innocent, the vulnerable, the marginalized? Who is best able to clothe the naked, the homeless, to teach the illiterate, to reach that young boy in the inner city — there are now so many who were raised without a father, without a male role model, without a strong marriage-based family, maybe not knowing anyone who has a father? Who is best able to reach that scared and frightened and scorned teenage girl who has just found out that she has become pregnant out of wedlock? Who is best able to wipe away the tear of the AIDS victim who huddles against the cold wind of a family's rejection? Who is best able to do that? Catholic teaching has a great deal to say on that issue.

In Washington, it is called the *devolution revolution*. The idea of taking the powers and responsibilities that have been centered in Washington for the last fifty years and sending them back to communities, state governments, local governments, to private charities, to churches, to synagogues, and to private individuals and allowing those entities to be more effective at meeting those needs. Pope Pius XI said it far better than any political leader has ever said it. He said it in an encyclical over sixty years ago:

> Just as it is gravely wrong to take from individuals what they can accomplish by their own initiative and industry and give it to the community, so also it is an injustice and at the same time a grave evil and disturbance of right order to assign to a greater and higher association what lesser and subordinate organizations can do. (*Quadragesimo anno*, 79; 1931)

That Catholic notion of subsidiarity is an unshakable and essential principle not only of Catholic social teaching, but of all that made America great. You know this wilderness was not settled by a department of covered wagons out of Washington, D.C. I don't know how many of you noticed, but did you notice that the world still turned and our lives still functioned even though the federal government shut down for five days in 1995? How many of you knew that mothers still got up in the morning and fixed their children breakfast? How many of you knew that fathers still read bedtime stories to wide-eyed children? How many of you knew that there still was somebody to rock his little baby to sleep on his chest? How many of you knew that on that particular Sunday there were still 130 million people who filled our churches?

The Hope of America

We are the most religiously devout nation in the world and I think it gives us hope that there are more people in church and at Mass on Sunday morning than are watching *60 Minutes* on Sunday night. And that is the hope of America.

There is no better example, really, of this principle of people fired by faith in God and by love for their fellow men and women — being able to meet the needs of a society better than any central government can — than the success, really the miracle, of the Catholic educational system in America. Parochial schools have a 95 percent graduation rate; public schools have a fifty-five percent graduation rate. Parochial schools have five percent of their money go to administration and overhead. In the public school system, half of all the money that we are spending every year, $325 billion, never even makes it into the classroom. In the parochial schools they teach young people, who score, by the way, on average, 170 points higher on their SATs, with $1,900 per pupil as opposed to the $5,200 per pupil that the public school system spends. I believe that the day is coming when every parent in America, regardless of religion, regardless of race, regardless of ethnic background, ought to be able to receive a scholarship or voucher so that they can send their child to the best school for that child, whether it's private, public, or parochial.

It is this very secular world view, this militantly secular world view, that is growing increasingly hostile to religion as it intrudes on what Richard John Neuhaus correctly called "The Naked Public Square," that believes that the government is God and that we are its servants. You and I represent a faith-based world view that argues that God is the author of our liberty, that men and women are created in His image, and that we are endowed in the words of the Declaration of Independence with certain inalienable rights. The sole purpose of God establishing government is to protect those God-given rights. And I'll tell you something, the first of those rights, the foundation of those rights, is the right to life, and we will not rest until every child is once again safe in his or her mother's womb.

National Right to Life and the Christian Coalition have been working together in pushing the partial-birth abortion ban. I believe that this will be, to the tragedy and the scourge and the unspeakable horror of abortion, what Grenada was to the fall of the Soviet empire. People ridiculed it when Grenada was liberated, but the truth of the matter is, it was the first time since the Bolshevik Revolution of 1917 that a single inch of soil anywhere in the world was liberated from communism. That partial-birth abortion bill will represent the first time that there has ever been a national law that banned a procedure that took the life of an innocent child in his or her mother's womb.

Cultural Change

And the truth is that none of what is happening, none of this revolution, is just a political revolution; it is a cultural change in society. You know Winston Churchill, who I think was the best friend that the American people ever had, foreign or domestic, once said, "The American people always do the right thing, after they have exhausted every other possibility." We have exhausted every other possibility, haven't we? We tried the sexual revolution. We tried "if it feels good, do it." We tried "I'm okay, you're okay."

We tried materialism and inquisitiveness. We tried filling our lives with the possessions and the rudiments of success. And what we discovered as a society is what every other society has discovered: You cannot fill what Pascal called the God-shaped vacuum that is in every person's soul with anything except the personal relationship with Jesus Christ and His Father.

So it's not just a political change; it is more deeply a spiritual shift that is shifting the plates of the American political landscape, and Catholics have been at the very center of that. According to Network Exit Polls that were taken on election day 1994, for the first time in American history, Roman Catholics, a majority of them, 56 percent of frequently church-attending Catholics, 51 percent of all Catholics, voted Republican in an off-year election. I believe that just as the Evangelicals have become the base vote of the Republican Party, Catholics today are now the swing vote in American politics. Any candidate who wins the Catholic vote will be able to govern America. No President has been elected, since John F. Kennedy was elected in 1960, without winning the Catholic vote. Richard Nixon won it in 1968 and 1972; Jimmy Carter barely carried it in 1976; Ronald Reagan and George Bush carried it throughout the 1980's; and Bill Clinton carried it, a plurality, not a majority, but a plurality of the Catholic vote in 1992. The Catholic vote holds the key to the future of America. I believe that if they can unite, if Catholics can unite with the Evangelical Christians, the Protestants who share their views on the sanctity of innocent human life, on the need for religious liberty and school choice and common sense values, I believe if Catholics and Evangelicals can unite, there is no person that can run for office in any city or any state in America that can't be elected. There is no bill that can't be passed in either House of Congress, or any state legislative chamber anywhere in America. It is the emerging force in the electorate today.

Anti-Catholicism

How historic that truly is, because I don't need to tell you that there was a time when major political parties in this country in the nineteenth century actually had anti-Catholic planks in their platform. It was not until 1928 that a Catholic was nominated by either major political party, and he was defeated in the campaign in which bigots made his Catholic religion the main issue. The truth is this — Catholicism never has been, is not today, and never will be a threat to American democracy. It was and remains the most colorful and the most vibrant thread running through the tapestry of American democracy.

Cardinal Gibbons said this: "No constitution is more in harmony with Catholic principles than the American constitution and no religion is more in accord with that constitution than the Catholic religion." And when people have tried to exclude Catholics or other people of faith from political life, we have answered in the words of John F. Kennedy, who as a Catholic, stood before the Houston Ministerial Association on September 12, 1960. A Catholic running for President, the first time since Alfred E. Smith experienced the bigotry of 1928, John Kennedy said this: "If 40 million Americans have lost their right to be President of the United States of America on the day they were baptized, then not only am I the loser, but this entire nation is the loser in the eyes of history and in the eyes of the world." And the tragedy today is that most of the bigotry directed at Evangelicals and Catholics doesn't come from the right as it did then. It now comes from the left. Who could forget the Art Exhibit funded by the National Endowment for the Arts just a few years ago. It referred to Cardinal John O'Connor as a fat cannibal and referred to St. Patrick's Cathedral as a house of walking swastikas on Fifth Avenue. That kind of bigotry has no place in American life and I do not believe that tax dollars should ever be used to attack the deeply held religious beliefs of any American, Catholic or Protestant.

When Clarence Thomas was nominated to the U. S. Supreme Court in 1991, the media was horrified to discover that he had been educated by nuns and they began to go out and investigate whether or not that might not be a problem if he got on the highest court in the land. Doug Wilder, the then Democratic Governor of Virginia, actually gave an interview in which he said, "The question about Clarence Thomas really isn't his constitutional views. The question is how much allegiance does he have to the Pope?" Can you imagine? Can you imagine that being said in America today? Of course what they didn't know was that he attended an Episcopal Church in Northern Virginia. It was just the fact that he had once been educated by Catholics that was the problem. And recently, Disney, through its subsidiary Miramax, distributed the film "Priest," which portrayed the Catholic priesthood as an order dominated by adulterers, moral reprobates, and homosexuals. And I want you to know that as Evangelicals we stand shoulder to shoulder with you, ensuring that never again will such bigotry be directed against Catholics and their religion, or be used to try and silence them and drive them from the public square. You ought to be welcomed into the political life of our nation. Faith in God isn't what's wrong with America; it is what's right with America. We ought to be encouraging people with faith in God to get more involved instead of ridiculing them and attacking them in the media and in our political discourse.

Catholic Alliance

I think you know that we have recently launched a division of the Christian Coalition called the Catholic Alliance, which is designed to formalize and continue to build bridges in our partnership with Roman Catholics. The Catholic Alliance, like the Catholic Campaign, is a lay movement. It consists of Catholic laity who are dedicated to the sanctity of innocent human life, who are dedicated to religious liberty and civil rights for all Americans, who are dedicated to ensuring that every child can attend the school of their choice, and who are dedicated to commonsense values. But the Catholic Alliance isn't all that we're doing. The truth is that 16 percent of the members of the Christian Coalition already today are Roman Catholics, according to internal surveys that we have conducted. My chief lobbyist here in Washington, Brian Lopina, is a Roman Catholic. Maureen Roselli who is the Director of the Catholic Alliance is here and, of course, she's Catholic. Brian's top deputy and our number two lobbyist in Washington is a Roman Catholic, and the person who drafted, wrote, and edited our Contract with the American Family graduated from Notre Dame University. In fact, if anybody knows any evangelicals who might be looking for a job, please give me their resumé, because we need at least one token evangelical in our Washington office.

But the truth is, you and I are uniting. Why are we uniting? We are uniting because the darkness has become so pervasive that the light must come together. We are coming together because whatever theological differences there are, there is far more that unites us and brings us together. Of course, we acknowledge that we have been separated as people of faith by a century-long chasm of distrust and suspicion. (I know this well from my study of history. When I was getting a Ph.D. in American history and had hoped to teach, you may find this hard to believe, but there are some people who wish that I was still teaching history!) The good news is that chasm is being bridged and those walls are crumbling. I believe that it is not the work of any man; I believe that it is the work of God. I believe that He is ushering in a new world and that is why we were so thrilled to join with Charles Colson and Richard John Neuhaus and Bill Bright with Campus Crusade for Christ in supporting the Evangelicals and Catholics Uniting Together project. It is bringing us together to work on the things that we care so deeply about.

Let me close with a quote from the Pope when he was at the United Nations during his visit to the United States in 1995. He said:

> We have within us the capacity for wisdom, for virtue and for mercy. With these gifts and with the help of God's grace we can build in the next century and in the next millennium a

civilization worthy of the human person. A true culture of freedom, and in doing so, we shall see that the tears of this century have watered the ground for a new springtime of the human spirit. We have lived in the bloodiest century in the history of humankind. We have seen the defeat, one in a hot war and the other in a cold war, of the twin evils of fascism and communism. . . .

If the Pope is right, and I believe he is, then those tears and that tragedy have prepared the way for us to usher in a new moment. A new moment for Catholics and Protestants as he said, "A springtime of the human experience."

We've got a lot of work to do. Let's go out and do it and let's do it with arms locked, united.

Catholics in the 104th Congress

The Catholic Church has been known as the Democratic party at prayer and was the party of the majority of the last election. There are 128 Catholics in the House, and that is seven more than two years ago. The Senate has twenty-one Catholics; that is a shift from twenty-three in 1992. Ten of those who voted pro-life are what we call the cafeteria Catholics. They choose what teachings they will observe and leave the rest. My little state of Illinois has eight Catholics, five of whom are pro-life and three are not.

My own feeling is that if we had the Catholics behind us in the pro-life movement in Congress, we would always carry the day. Instead we are struggling in hand-to-hand combat with not a great many battles really won. We had to tragically recede from the only exception to abortion that we would tolerate federal funding for, and that was the life of the mother. We could not prevail a few years ago with that single exception. The rape and incest exceptions had to be folded in. That created enormous controversy because there is no justification for killing an unborn child other than simply where the life of the mother would be forfeited. Where you have a choice, certainly the child created though the criminal acts rape or incest has not committed a crime and ought not to receive capital punishment, which the courts have said is too disproportionate a punishment for the aggressor. On the other hand, you're faced with a very difficult problem. The aim of the pro-life movement ought to be to save the maximum number of lives politically feasible. About one half of one percent of the abortions, and even pregnancies, are the result of either rape and incest, and so you put at risk 99.5 percent to remain pristine as to the half of one percent. When you have a house burning down and you cannot save everybody, you save as many as you can and you make the practical political judgment, but it is an agonizing one to yield on those exceptions for the purpose of saving the lives of the other 99.5 percent. I hope the day comes when we have enough muscle in the House and in the Senate to go back to the simple life of the mother exception, but we don't right now.

The Leadership of the Holy Father

At the United Nations in 1995 we saw the moral and spiritual leaders of the world speaking to humanity and for humanity as no one else can today. At Giants Stadium we saw an incredible display of fervor as over 80,000 Catholics stood for hours in the drenching rain in order to celebrate Mass with the Vicar of Christ. A similar piety was evident at the recitation of the Rosary at St. Patrick's Cathedral and at the Mass at Baltimore's Camden Yards. The Holy Father touched the lives and hearts of Catholics in America in a very singular way. We owe him a debt of gratitude. He is indeed a Father and a friend.

Did what he have to say bear on the works of Catholics and Congress? Yes. When at Giants Stadium the Pope called on America to be a hospitable society, he adopted an image from the right-to-life movement. In pro-life work the hospitable-society image has served two purposes. First, it helps us make clear that abortion-on-demand violates the basic trajectory of American life, which is one of broadening the boundaries of the community of common protection and concern. Second, in addition to its lethal effects on the unborn and its degrading effects on women and men, the abortion license has become a serious public consequence for our society. The Holy Father made this plain when he linked the abortion license to the pro-euthanasia agitation in our country and to the breakdown in family life. Abortion has never been and never can be a matter of private choice alone. If our society cannot find the means to protect the weakest and most vulnerable among us, we shall have abandoned the American promise of justice for all. And that's why abortion is the great civil rights issue of our time. And that's why I must take respectful exception to a formulation in the United States Catholic Conference's new statement on political responsibility in the forthcoming election year. Speaking in the name of the Bishops, the Conference document says this:

> We stand with the unborn and the undocumented when the politicians seem to be abandoning them. We defend children in the womb and on welfare. We oppose the violence of abortion and the vengeance of capital punishment.

I'll leave the substance of the issues of immigration reform, welfare reform, and capital punishment for another day. They are important issues; they are controversial. But I do regret the suggestion of moral equivalence contained in the form of the United States Catholic Conference statement. The Holy Father in his addresses in the United States did not suggest that the abortion license, which takes one and a half million innocent lives every year, is one issue among many. No, he argued quite rightly, this is the great moral challenge in America today. There are other challenges, to be sure, but the issue of the right to life of the unborn cuts to the heart of the American experiment like no other issue. I'm afraid this is more than a mere stylistic difference of opinion; it's an affirmation of the seamless-garment metaphor, which is based on, in my opinion, an unwarranted moral equivalence.

A Hospitable Society

In the 104th Congress we tried to give legal meaning to the image of America as a hospitable society by our pro-life legislative efforts, and I would argue also that the renewal of America as a land of mutual responsibility is also advanced when we return considerable authority over education, welfare, and other social policies to the states. There is no reason that America will renew itself as a hospitable society through the workings of the federal bureaucracy. No, the fantastic reach of that bureaucracy into every nook and cranny of our lives has helped erode the tissue of our civil society. Rebuilding a hospitable, responsible America will take place primarily at the local level, by getting the federal government out of the way of local initiative. We in the Congress are seeking to rebuild America as that hospitable society.

The social doctrine of John Paul II has consistently urged that all Catholics live in solidarity with the poor. Compassion for the poor is a classic Christian virtue. Compassion wasn't invented by political parties, and the parable of the good Samaritan did not come out of a political focus group. What has been boldly innovative about the Holy Father's social doctrine is his insistence that we give effect to our compassion for the poor, not by encouraging dependency on a new welfare plantation, but by empowering the poor to participate in social and economic life. That's the purpose of the welfare-reform legislation that's been making its way painfully through Congress. We want to break the cycle of welfare dependency. We want to remove incentives to counterproductive behavior, but an essential parallel to those concerns is that state and local governments and independent agencies like the Church, especially the Church, work with those now stuck on the welfare plantation so that our fellow Americans can become, as the Pope often puts it, artisans of their own destinies. In his homily at Baltimore's Camden Yards, the Holy Father challenged Americans to live our freedom so that freedom finds its fulfillment in goodness. We can get government out of the way of that process of modern renewal. We can reverse the policies that have indeed encouraged immorality, but the moral renewal of American's democracy is going to be the people's job, not the government's job. That's why groups like the Catholic Campaign for America are so important. You can do in your neighborhoods, cities, and states what we in Washington can only encourage. You can work to restore a spirit of neighborliness and mutual responsibility to our community. You can create a great groundswell of support for parental choice and education. You can teach your children. As the Pope put it, freedom is not a matter of doing whatever we like; freedom is the right to do what we ought.

The Catholic community in America has a singular responsibility. Pope John Paul II has, over the past five years, articulated what is arguably the world's most sophisticated moral case for democracy and the world's most scathing criticism of the functioning of established democracies. If Catholics in America really got to know the social doctrine of this remarkable Pope, if they made his teachings the centerpiece intellectually and ethically in their approach to public life, then we would, I'm convinced, see a great renewal of the American democratic experience. We all should try to do our part, but the energy for renewal must be generated by the people, and I can think of no more energizing vision of the free, virtuous, and responsible society than that given to us by Pope John Paul II.

The degree to which we make that vision our own will determine the future of the Catholic effort to build an America worthy of its great promise.

A Call to Catholic Citizens

I serve as Chairman of the International Operations and Human Rights Committee in Congress and for the past sixteen years I, along with others, have pushed hard to secure religious freedom around the world — and an end to torture and abuse of believers, who are persecuted for their faith.

I've not only read the accounts of heroes of our faith in books like Romanian Pastor Richard Wurmbrand's *Tortured for Christ* and Cuba's Armando Valladares' *Against All Hope*, but I've led several human rights missions to China, the Soviet Union, Romania, the Baltics, the Balkans, Eastern Europe, and other nations. I've met for hours on end with persecuted believers and their persecutors to press for freedom of religion and an end to the persecution.

On one human rights trip to Romania in 1985, Congressman Frank Wolf of Virginia and I demanded the release of numerous imprisoned pastors and believers, including Father Gheorghe Calciu. We succeeded. At a press conference after his release, Father Calciu quietly told of his many years of suffering for Christ, then finished by telling how the dreaded secret police known as the "Securitate," decided to kill him by putting two common thugs in his cell with instructions to end his life — in exchange for a reduced sentence. Father Calciu, undeterred and ever the missionary, preached the Gospel of Christ to these hardened men, and both gave their lives to the Lord. When their sentences were extended rather than shortened for failing to perform the deed for which they were recruited, they went right on praising God — having found the Truth that set them free.

I heard similar miraculous stories in Perm Camp 35 in Russia, in the late 1980's. Mr. Wolf and I — after two years of negotiation — were the first parliamentarians to get into that infamous gulag. We not only interviewed each prisoner of conscience, but gave them Bibles. I'll never forget seeing the tears of joy flowing down the faces of many of these saints, as they clutched the Bibles close to their hearts. I was amazed that these prisoners weren't filled with malice or hatred toward their KGB captors — but with love and forgiveness.

On one of three human rights trips to the People's Republic of China, I heard breathtaking stories of the Christian House Church Movement and oppressed Catholics. One Christian woman — with tears in her eyes — told me how she had been forcibly aborted by crude and rough family planning cadres, as part of the PRC's one-child per couple policy, and that she prayed that her baby was in Heaven. Yet, like Christ, she said she forgave them — for they "knew not what they had done." I was amazed.

Another told how a public security policeman beat, harassed, and robbed Christians. Well, his wife who was blind converted — and was healed of her blindness. That police officer — like the Roman jailor in our Lord's day — converted as well. Such is the power and mercy of the God that we serve.

In Matthew's Gospel, Jesus admonished us to care for the persecuted, the hungry, those in prison — the "least of our brethren." For me, this means being absolutely serious about human rights and the protection of all who are weak, disenfranchised, or vulnerable. For me this means inclusion of all people — regardless of race, sex, age, or condition of dependency, including unborn babies whose right to life is cruelly denied by some nations — including our own. Human rights are indivisible.

Today, millions of Christians and others of good will endure torture and humiliation for their faith. It is our responsibility to speak out on their behalf — and to make sure our government utilizes all means available to secure their freedom — whether it be a humane refugee policy or the linkage of human rights with trade or other means of statecraft. We must do all to assist all persecuted brethren.

Moral Relativism

Contrast the strength of character of our persecuted brethren — who daily risk their lives and professions and often languish in gulags for their faith — with the person described in the following story.

One day Nikita Khrushchev went into a Soviet factory and asked one of the factory workers whether or not he believed in God. The worker thought for a moment and replied, "At home, yes; here at work, no."

When it comes to advancing fundamental moral values in the public square, does that kind of duality ever describe us? "At home, I'm a tiger; in public, well, I'm a pussycat." Do we tend to take a walk when we should speak out? Do we let someone else do it?

Lincoln once said "to sin by silence when they should protest makes cowards of men." Does that describe us — always, never, or from time to time?

Modern public officials seem to be applauded — even rewarded — for *failing* to uphold fundamental moral values in public policy. The liberal media goes out of its way to praise those who routinely deposit what they claim to be their core moral beliefs in the nearest trash can prior to setting foot in the Congress, a mayor's office, a state legislature, or the White House.

Public officials who practice this duality are regarded as tolerant and open-minded. The ones who stick to their guns on moral principle are neanderthals, myopic, and even bigots.

Yet, we know what our Lord thinks about wishy-washy, lukewarm people — especially when a culture is in the clutches of a moral meltdown. Dante, too, had few kind things to say about those who choose neutrality in time of crisis.

All of us, on occasion, pledge to do one thing and end up doing precisely the opposite. Thankfully, St. Paul suggests, that as flawed humans, such backsliding is part of our human condition; but it is correctable.

This condition of our soul, we are taught, is fixed by allowing

God's grace to re-make us. And inspire us. And lead us. And give us courage, hope, and love.

Many people in our time claim that they are personally opposed to abortion, but, in the public domain, they stampede in retreat when challenged to put an end to America's child holocaust.

Society — especially Hollywood and the liberal press — demands that we not "impose our morality" on anyone else; good morality is relative, arbitrary, elective, and capricious. It's all in the eye of the beholder, after all. There are no moral absolutes.

Of course, such an obtuse view is the antithesis of Christianity, and a recipe for personal and collective failure. And when an entire society — or major element of it — embraces this view, the moral fabric of a nation is shredded and eventually destroyed.

The myriad of immoral policies that collectively form the zeitgeist of America in 1996 — undergirded by bad law and aggressively promoted with taxpayer subsidy — are the bitter fruits of the moral relativism that took deep root in the 1960's.

A Moral Cause

I'll never forget one of my Congressional campaigns back in the 1980's when a smart and sophisticated opponent I was running against tried to frame the whole right-to-life issue as one of "Chris Smith thinks that somehow he is morally superior to the rest of us." I'm a fellow struggling sinner, just like everyone else. Thankfully, we have the redemptive blood of Jesus Christ and the wonderful sacrament of reconciliation available to us. As believers we do believe in reconciliation. All of us have fallen short of the glory of God, as it says in the Scriptures; but it was a very clever way of trying to dismiss our deeply held convictions as smug, self-righteous, and petty. And you know that kind of attack works very effectively against many people. They back off and are neutralized.

My response was that our position — not me — *our position*

123

of defending the unborn, the least of our brethren in the words of our Lord, is morally right. The act of dismembering and chemically poisoning baby girls and boys is morally wrong. I have no doubt about that. The child abuse that is entailed in killing unborn children and the unbelievable misery that is visited upon women who have abortions tells me we're right. I make no apology for candor. If we can't assert that abortion is wrong and our court-imposed policy is a national scandal, how then can we condemn and legislate against other evils like murder, robbery, or rape? Women who support abortion need our love and compassion, and some of our most outspoken, articulate, and compassionate spokeswomen are the women who have actually had abortions. We welcome them with open arms. The pro-life movement is a non-judgmental movement, but we do make judgments about the rightness and wrongness of abortion itself. And it is a cruel deed — a sickening form of child abuse that leads to other abuses.

In the years since *Roe* v. *Wade*, we have had exponential rises in child abuse, and the pundits wonder why. We wonder why there are 24,000 to 25,000 murders in this country every year and escalating crime of every sort. It is all because we have, as Pope John Paul II calls it, a Culture of Death, where we not only tolerate or acquiesce, but we actually endorse and promote the killing of unborn children, and that leads to a whole series of bad consequences.

Mother Teresa has said, "The greatest destroyer of peace is abortion." It used to be that the womb was the greatest sanctuary a child could have. Now it has become a tomb — the end of the road on earth — for so many children. When the pro-abortion crowd says to a child, "You're unwelcomed; we don't care about you; we're going to treat you like a disease or an object and kill you with abortion," we cannot pretend to be bewildered as to why our society has become so dysfunctional. I do think that the lynchpin for ushering back those moral values that many of us crave, is reinstating legal protection for the unborn. We can make progress on many fronts — confront every bad policy and moral wrong, but

124

if abortion on demand remains the law of our land, progress elsewhere will likely be minimal.

Core Values

Congressman Henry Hyde gave a very insightful speech not so long ago to a new crop of freshman lawmakers. He noted that everyone was properly enthusiastic about their elections to Congress, about their plans, and how they're going to do this and that. Yet, he struck a seemingly discordant but sobering note when he said: "I want all of you to think about what it is that you are willing to lose your seat over. What are your core values? What are you willing to fight for? Are your convictions deep enough to be willing to pay the price of being ousted in the next election? Or will you capitulate?" These were provocative, basic questions from one of the best and most respected lawmakers in the country. It's a line of questioning that begs our thought and prayer.

Unlike our persecuted brethren in the gulag — have any of us resisted, as the Bible says, to the point of shedding blood? Many politicians run for the hills when they get a bad editorial. If they can't stand the heat we should vote them out of the kitchen.

We live in a free society, and as such, have moral responsibilities as citizens that are not easily satisfied. You and I are responsible for what's going on in Congress, the White House, and at all levels of government. We have to make it our business and not somebody else's to make the difference. I wouldn't mind walking away or taking a break sometimes from the extremely unpleasant issue of abortion. I hate abortion. I hate it with a passion. I hate talking about it. I hate the methods of violence — chemical poisoning, literal dismemberment of the baby's body, and the newest method that's being promoted that Congress sought to outlaw but Clinton continued, the partial-birth abortion. This grisly method of slaughtering babies puts in sharp focus and brings new light and scrutiny to the dark and dirty secret of the abortion industry — the actual violent act of abortion.

No more cover-up. No more euphemisms about choice. The cheap sophistry that insults our intelligence is ending. In the partial-birth abortion, the so-called doctor — baby butcher is more precise — actually sucks the brains out of a child's head in order to kill the child. Anyone with eyes and an open mind can see that this is child abuse. This is not a compassionate act, or a fundamental liberty or free choice. And it must be stopped. I long for the day when we won't have to talk about abortion or work against it because the child's life is protected. But in good conscience neither you nor I can walk away from it now or anytime soon. Why? Because we deeply care for both mothers and children. It is because we care about, as the Lord said, the least of our brethren, that we go to the mat.

I strongly believe that each of us needs to respond to the call to action now. No more delays. Please! The sleeping giant — the Catholic Church — must become more active and more energized on the pro-life issue than ever before. The electorate must become informed and mobilized in defense of life. We must recognize that the moral health of our nation is at stake and begin voting for these core values. Pocketbook issues are very important — but the sanctity of life supercedes money. It is all a matter of votes when you get down to it.

I'll never forget the national healthcare debate. Passage was a given — a sure bet — during the first year of Mr. Clinton's presidency. What stopped it was not the cost, not the muddle of details about it; it was the right-to-life issue. Bill Clinton tried to legislate abortion on demand as a "mandated benefit" and force all premium payers, all taxpayers, all employers to pay for it. Former Congressman Jack Kemp always said, "If you subsidize something, you get more of it." If all of a sudden we're making abortion as easy as having one's tonsils removed, and have an expanding pool of abortionists plying their wicked craft, the result would be more abortions. Such a policy would further trivialize the sanctity of human life.

But let me say it was the Catholic Church and our friends in other denominations that put a tourniquet on abortion expansion. As a matter of fact, Tom Foley who was then the Speaker of the House, made an incredible statement. He said he would not even bring the bill up unless he could bring it up under what we call a closed rule, which would have precluded any amendments from being offered to it. We prepared several amendments which would have stripped out the abortion mandate and ensured that there was a workable conscientious objection wherein individuals and institutions could refuse, including Catholic hospitals, to be a part of this inhumane business. Mr. Foley soon discovered that he could not get the votes needed to bring up a closed rule — and decided to spike so-called healthcare reform altogether.

1996 Crucial to Unborn

In 1996 the stakes couldn't be higher and the challenge before us demands immediate action. We are at a crossroads. In the 1994 elections, not a single pro-lifer was defeated, Democrat or Republican. I would submit to you that it may be difficult, but not impossible to replicate that standard in '96 or any other future election. Today, the pursuit of social justice and the promotion of righteousness summons men and women of character to run for office and to urge their political parties to respect life. There are major differences in the major party platforms, and I'm going to work vigorously to ensure the Republican platform does not backtrack. That would be a travesty. I must say to those in my party who are seeking to undermine the GOP's pro-life plank and water down efforts to protect life, that I respect you as individuals, but the undeniable consequence of your position is dead babies and injured women. We can't let that happen.

And to my Democrat friends — cease being the official party of abortion on demand. You dishonor your rich tradition of looking out for the little guy when you tout abortion so brazenly and in such an extreme way in your party's national set of basic principles — your party platform. Follow the courageous leadership of Governor Bob Casey. Be inclusive — and save the children.

We need to pray, fast, and work tirelessly for a Congress and a President that respect the sanctity of human life. This generation of kids and their moms are vulnerable and need friends. If these were your children or mine, how hard would we fight for them? Would you or I be so uninterested and indifferent about a candidate's abortion position — well, he's good on the other issues — if it resulted in the loss of *our* child? I think not!

The Defining Issue

I submit to you that the abortion issue is the defining issue of our time. We must take seriously the words of our Lord, "Whatsoever you do to the least of my brethren, you do likewise to Me." And that message, as the Pope and Bishops have so eloquently said, must apply to every facet of our lives, especially in politics. We can't be like that factory worker who said, at home I believe, but in the workplace I'm not going to touch it. It means that pro-life politicians have to be faithful and make protection of the unborn a priority. No more backroom sellouts. Inconvenience comes with the territory — endure some flak for the sake of the children. And yes, there are times when you may have to compromise, when you get the best deal you can, but it had better be based on principle, and it better be the very best deal that you can get.

I hope that Catholic colleges, high schools, and elementary schools will become more serious about promoting the value of life. Many of our future leaders are being molded in those institutions. Let's work to ensure that they emerge with a determination and a vision to challenge the dominant secular culture rather than conform to it. I sometimes wonder if Heaven looks at least a bit askance when prestigious schools like Georgetown and Notre Dame and some of our great colleges care more about their basketball and football teams — don't get me wrong, I love sports — than raising up men and women of moral and ethical character who will challenge the prevailing anti-life mores of our time. When freshly minted doctors and lawyers graduate from Catholic institutions of higher learning — what drum do they march to? Will they bend with the wind or into it? My wife, Marie, our four children, and I were privileged to be, as were a lot of other people, in Sacred Heart Cathedral in Newark when Pope John Paul II came and gave a magnificent sermon. He touched all of us with his holiness and with his goodness. Well, President Clinton — the Abortion President — was there as well, sitting four or five seats in front of my family. I watched him, as I have during the last three years, and the man is unbelievable. Like a chameleon, he was as Catholic as anybody else in that church. And when the President and Mrs. Clinton exited down the middle aisle, they got a thunderous standing ovation despite his outrageous anti-child policies. The thought crossed my mind, "My God, in '96 he's going to win the Catholic vote again." After all, according to post-election polling in '92, Bill Clinton is President, promoting his immoral pro-abortion agenda from the White House, precisely because of the Catholic vote. We put him in over the top and into office.

We've got to take seriously that there are consequences to the men and women we put into positions of authority.

Even a cursory review of Bill Clinton's record shows he is obsessed with promoting abortion. For example, by Executive Order the President repealed pro-life Title X regulations that had prohibited abortion counseling and referrals in federally funded family planning clinics. He repealed the moratorium on the harvesting of brain and other tissues from aborted babies. He repealed the ban on abortions in overseas military hospitals. He repealed the Mexico City policy that denied funds to organizations that perform or promote abortions overseas like International Planned Parenthood Federation based in London that received a $75 million grant. He greased the skids for testing of RU-486 — the French abortion pill. He reversed asylum for victims of forced abortion in China (many of whom are in our jails awaiting deportation). And he reversed the Reagan-Bush boycott of organizations like the U.N. Population Fund that support or comanage coercive population control programs. He used taxpayer funds to pay for thousands of abortions on demand in several federal programs and tried to repeal the Hyde Amendment, which survived in a weakened form. He pushed the so-called Freedom of Choice Act that went beyond *Roe* v. *Wade*. He pushed and signed into law the Freedom of Access to Clinic Entrances Act which targets and singles out pro-lifers for harsh criminal and civil penalties for peaceful protest. And with the stroke of his pen, he empowered abortionists to continue doing partial-birth abortions, even as a method of birth control. *Every* judicial and executive appointment went to pro-abortionists — yes, there is a rigid litmus test — except his Ambassador to the Vatican, which I guess was a nice touch to some.

I was in Beijing for the Women's Conference and I was also in Cairo for the Population Conference when this Administration was in the lead pushing an international right to abortion, not to mention other policies that violate biblical morality. There are 95 to 100 countries around the world that safeguard their unborn child from the moment of conception, virtually all of Central and South America as well as Ireland and the Philippines. They are now under siege — Brazil, Peru, Paraguay, countries all over the globe that protect their unborn children — as a result of the Clinton Administration working in tandem with the International Planned Parenthood Federation of London and others in the multi-million dollar pro-abortion industry. These folks are relentless — and toxic. The Clinton Administration is pushing population control and undermining the family all over the world. The "tools" of legitimate, economic, and humanitarian aid, refinancing and rescheduling of debt are being used to coerce countries to adopt aggressive population control policies and to reverse protections for their unborn children. A pro-lifer in the White House and pro-life additions in Congress — especially in the

Senate — can help halt this dangerous cultural imperialism that gives new meaning to the "ugly American."

Prayer

We need to pray. We need to fast. We need to work as we've never worked before at every level to reform our society and to do what we must do to — as I said before — wake up the sleeping giant, the Catholic Church. And we shouldn't point fingers and say the Bishops need to do more. Believe me our Church leaders have been in this fight and they have the lumps to prove it. We — the laity — are the Church. And we need to do our part.

It is sad but true that most of the Catholics in the House and the Senate are pro-abortion. Yes, that's right. Catholics constitute the largest block of people affiliated with one faith in the Congress, and the majority of Catholics in both the House and the Senate turn out to be pro-abortion. I don't judge their character; I don't judge their motives; I don't judge their hearts. That's up to the Almighty. But their actions as lawmakers kill countless children and put their mothers at risk. Tens of millions are dead and bleeding as a result. And on a global scale, the pro-life policies of entire countries are in jeopardy because of our Abortion President, his vast bureaucracy, and his minions in the Congress and in the courts.

Wise as Serpents, Gentle as Doves

I used to be a Democrat. I left the party two decades ago after someone showed me the door because of my pro-life beliefs. There is however a remnant of pro-life Democrats, people like Congressman Jim Oberstar of Minnesota, Harold Volkmer of Missouri, Alan Mollohan of West Virginia, and the indefatigable Governor Bob Casey of Pennsylvania, who are steadfast and take it on the chin for their convictions, especially from their own party elite. So those of you who happen to be Democrats, make

defending the defenseless a priority issue for your party. Take it
back — it's been stolen — and put the thieves to flight. Reverse
the stranglehold the militant abortionists have on the Democrats.
We need to be bipartisan, and we also need to be absolutely clear
that we're not going to be snowed anymore because some
politicians can talk a good game, sound pro-life but do otherwise.
Jimmy Carter, when he was trying to win the Iowa Caucus, sent a
strong signal that he was pro-life, and this was crucial to his
eventual success. It was, as we all know now, a lie. Senator Tom
Harkin of Iowa did much the same thing. As have many others
since. And perhaps one of the biggest lies of all, Bill Clinton wants
us to believe he's trying to make abortion "rare."

We need to be as wise as serpents, yet gentle as doves as our
Lord says, and cut through the disinformation routinely served up
by deceitful politicians and a biased media.

Get to work, my friends. We haven't a moment to lose.
Commit yourselves — your talent and your treasure — and ask
God to guide and empower everything we think, say, and do in His
service on behalf of His precious ones.

Be Not Afraid:
Look the Adversary in the Eye

In July of 1864, the Civil War was far from over for people in Washington. A bold Confederate general named Jubal Early crossed the Potomac and led an unexpected attack on the nation's capital. President Abraham Lincoln wanted to see the action, so he traveled to Fort Stevens and mounted the parapet facing the battlefield. Southern riflemen were just 100 yards away — the length of a football field — firing volley after volley into the line of blue defenders. Amid them was an inviting target, the sixteenth President of the United States — standing six feet, four inches tall — wearing that famous top hat and making no attempt whatever to duck the bullets whizzing past him.

He looked the adversary right in the eye.

Everybody in a gray uniform knew who he was — but no one shot him. After a few seconds, a horrified Union officer yelled, "Get down, you fool!" then firmly escorted the President off the parapet. The officer was Captain Oliver Wendell Holmes, Jr., who would later serve on the U.S. Supreme Court.

Now, some people may think the President's action was rash — it was the only time in American history in which an American President has been under fire while in office. But deep down inside, Lincoln needed to see first-hand what he was fighting against — and to rededicate himself to what he was fighting for. As the war dragged on, more than 420 Americans were dying daily. Lincoln had to reaffirm that his faith, his morals, his policies, his conduct of the war — everything he believed in — were right before his Maker. He believed deeply in providence, and it was not lost on him that when he was standing on the parapet of Fort

Stevens, God chose not to take him from this earth. And sure enough, he lived just long enough to see the war's conclusion some nine months later.

I believe that this little story has a big moral for us today: It takes courage to look adversity in the face, to seek God's will, and to do the right thing, no matter what the cost. Everybody in this audience knows the battles we must fight today. Exhibit "A" is the *Index of Leading Cultural Indicators*, developed by one of the most courageous and articulate Catholics in the public square today, Bill Bennett.

Our nation is threatened along a front that is both broad and deep. Catholics in the public square are battling it out in Hollywood, in the nation's public schools, on college campuses, in front of abortion clinics, outside adult book stores, in the courts, in state legislatures, and on Capitol Hill. Despite the scale of the war, we have tremendous moral and spiritual armament upon which to draw. Our fortress is the Catholic Church; and the parapet on which we stand are her teachings. Our commander-in-chief is the Lord; and his able lieutenant — whose talents perfectly match the needs of our day — is the Holy Father.

When Pope John Paul II delivered his homily at Camden Yards on October 8, 1995, he talked about Lincoln and his vision of America. Echoing the author of the Gettysburg Address, he asked: Would our nation, "conceived in liberty," long endure?

Courage in the Public Square

It seems to me that we will only endure if we are guided by what might be called the "perennial principles." These include:

• respect for each human life *from the moment of conception* to *life's natural end*;

• commitment to freedom that is grounded in truth and personal responsibility;

• recognition of the family's central role in education and indeed all of life;

• and appreciation for the value of hard and honest work.

But something more is needed than the enunciation of principles, important as that is. As Catholics, we need to argue for them and instill them in the public square. We need to stand on the parapet and look the adversary in the eye. And that requires the old cardinal virtue of courage.

In thinking about public Catholicism in the next millennium, I would stress the courage, the boldness, we'll need to tackle all of the challenges out there.

Here we should take our lead from the Holy Father himself. In *Crossing the Threshold of Hope*, he says to us, again and again, echoing Scripture: "Be not afraid." As St. Paul wrote, "The Spirit God has given us is no cowardly Spirit." So — be not afraid.

Nor should we shrink from working with anyone who shares our values — be they Orthodox, Protestant, Jewish, Muslim, or members of other faiths and creeds — for they are working to build up the culture of life.

Death on Demand

Regarding the life issues, let me first say how proud I am to have served with Governor Robert Casey, and how honored I am to stand shoulder-to-shoulder with him as one of many solidly pro-life governors. Bob Casey is one of the most persistent and courageous men in America, and his "Campaign for the American Family," founded in October 1995, is making a significant contribution to building up what the Holy Father calls the "culture of life."

That's not politically correct in the era of *Roe* v. *Wade*. But pro-life forces are slowly but surely winning the war. We have won intellectually, we have won morally, and more and more we are

winning legislatively. As Senate Majority Leader back in 1988, I
helped lead the ballot fight to end taxpayer-funded Medicaid
abortions in Michigan — and it passed overwhelmingly. I hope
Governor Casey will visit us in Michigan because I think he'd
applaud our efforts to protect unborn babies.

During my first term as Governor, I signed two bills
restricting abortion — one requiring parental consent, the other a
twenty-four-hour waiting period. A third bill has been under
consideration in the Michigan legislature and it would make doing
deliberate harm to a wanted child in his or her mother's womb a
crime. I will sign this bill the minute it reaches my desk.

Our efforts on behalf of unborn children are beginning to
show results. In 1995, Michigan, I am proud to say, led the nation
in the percentage decrease in the number of abortions. Let me
repeat that: *In 1995, Michigan led the nation in the percentage
decrease in the number of abortions*. It's a trend I will do
everything in my power to reinforce.

This good news is offset by bad news that disturbs me deeply.
Jack Kevorkian, "Dr. Death," plies his ghoulish trade and claims
more victims. Mr. Kevorkian, whose medical license was revoked
by his peers in November of 1991, shows an appalling disregard for
ethics and professional standards. That betrays his real agenda,
which is to spread the "culture of death." Kevorkian would have
the culture of death become a way of life. Like those who support
abortion on demand, Kevorkian wants death on demand.

This preoccupation with death can also be seen in one of his
hobbies. It turns out that when Kevorkian is not helping
vulnerable men and women kill themselves in the back of a van, he
fancies himself a painter and holds exhibits of his so-called art.
One look at his paintings and you see that what he really has a
talent for is Catholic-bashing.

One of his most publicized paintings is called "Born Again." It
depicts Hitler in the heavens with his finger touching the
Michigan State Capitol. A parody of our state shows a priest
pointing to a rising sun on which is superimposed a swastika. It

reads, "The New Seal of the Loyal Papal State of Michigan 1991," and *"Engler über Alles."* It is ironic that the man who is devoting his life to finding better ways to kill people would try to link a Catholic, pro-life governor with Nazism.

If there is a silver lining in all of this, it's that Kevorkian is forcing citizens to choose which side they're on: the culture of life . . . or the culture of death.

Welfare Reform

In addition to helping citizens take a stand against abortion and assisted suicide, Catholic principles can and should animate other areas of public policy — for example, welfare reform. The Catholic Campaign for America released a major survey of Catholic positions on key issues. The results show that the overwhelming majority of Catholics polled — some seventy-six percent — believe that welfare as we know it has been a failure — and they are right. It's significant that the voting history of those surveyed is slightly more Democratic than Republican. For it confirms that both parties are unhappy with the Great Society. It has become all too apparent that much of the Great Society was a great mistake — and it certainly was neither good, nor great, for society.

Christ admonishes us to help the poor. But we do people no favor — in fact, we do them great harm — when we perpetuate a system that fosters dependence, discourages marriage, and punishes work. That's the system we've had for thirty years, and it leaves recipients hopeless.

St. Paul wrote:

> We were not idle when we were with you, we did not eat any one's bread without paying, but with toil and labor we worked night and day, that we might not burden any of you. . . . For even when we were with you, we gave you this command: If any one will not work, let him not eat. (2 Thess 3:7, 10)

You cannot get any clearer than that. And, using St. Paul as a guide, you could summarize Michigan's reforms with a single word

— work. I believe that the best welfare program in the world is a job. Everybody can and should contribute to the community. It's a principle that's perfectly consistent with the teachings of the Catholic Church.

But when I took office, Michigan's welfare policies were self-defeating and downright corrupting. Able-bodied men and women without children were getting government checks to sit at home. We began welfare reform in 1991 when we told 80,000 able-bodied single adults without children to get off the dole and get a job. To show we were serious, we didn't just reduce the program; we ended it.

Today, our welfare reform plan is going far beyond the termination of just one program. We are requiring all remaining welfare recipients with children to go to work. Currently, more than thirty percent of Michigan's AFDC clients are working and earning income — not in make-work jobs, but in private sector jobs. And we are working to increase that percentage. However, our thirty percent who are working compares to roughly eight percent nationwide.

Just as impressive, over the last two years, 70,000 Michigan families have made it off welfare rolls and on private payrolls. They're taking charge of their lives and earning enough money that they no longer qualify for cash assistance. The bottom line: Michigan's welfare caseload has fallen to its lowest level in a quarter-century.

That's the good news. The bad news is that Michigan has implemented welfare reform, not inspired by Washington, but in spite of Washington. Sure, the President has approved waivers, which have helped. But states shouldn't have to trek to Washington, hat in hand, begging federal bureaucrats to fix a broken system one waiver at a time.

Returning power and authority to the states is perfectly consistent with the Catholic principle of subsidiarity. A larger unit of government should not do what a smaller unit can, and no unit of government should do what civil society can. That's the principle of subsidiarity as defined by Pope Leo XIII and as upheld by Pope John Paul II.

States should have the freedom to end welfare as we know it — no strings attached. Fifty states finding creative ways to break the cycle of dependency is a far more compassionate strategy than today's system, which has led to despair in our cities, dissolution in our families, and dependence on our government. That's not compassionate.

Education Reform

But more is needed than just helping get people off welfare. We need to redouble our efforts to keep them from getting on welfare in the first place. And that means education reform. I have been a strong supporter of public schools, but I am also a strong supporter of reforming those schools. Public school reform must proceed from the premise that the first and best teachers of our children are Mom and Dad — and that you can trust Mom and Dad to send their children to the schools that best honor their values and meet their needs.

It is absolutely essential that we offer families more public school choices, and where state constitutions permit, choices that involve private and parochial schools as well. You may have heard Paul Harvey when he reported that wherever educational choice was offered on the ballot November 8, 1995, it passed overwhelmingly.

School choice is becoming an unstoppable movement — but it sure has been a long time in the making. Let me read to you something that was written by the twentieth-century's greatest Catholic historian, Christopher Dawson:

> In claiming the right to maintain separate schools and to teach its own principles to its own people, the [Catholic] Church is the champion of freedom in the most vital matter, and even the liberal democratic state is becoming totalitarian when it asserts the principle of the single school and claims a universal

monopoly of teaching. ("Civilization in Crisis," *Catholic World* 182; p. 252)

That was forty years ago — yet the words could have been written yesterday.

Michigan's constitution prohibits any direct or indirect type of voucher program or tuition tax credit. Yet, even with these rigid restraints, the education reform movement in our state has not been derailed. I am proud that we have the best charter school law in the nation. The law has been in effect only eighteen months, but forty-one charter schools are already up and running, giving families more choice in their children's education. I anticipate dozens more opening up their doors within the next couple of years.

These market-driven charter schools are having a profound effect on what has been a virtual monopoly of public education. Competition and choice are laying the foundation for an education renaissance in the twenty-first century. And this education renaissance is integral to our efforts to strengthen families, break the cycle of welfare dependency, and revitalize civil society.

Be Not Afraid

In closing, let me make two final points. First, Catholics have always recognized that there is a limit to what government can and should do. That is our great strength as we enter the public square and debate the issues of the day. We recognize that government cannot take the place of a mom or dad — and it certainly cannot replace God. But where there is a role for government, we must, in the words of former Michigan Governor George Romney, "Be bold."

Which leads to my second point. None of the reforms for which I've fought has been easy to achieve. In fact, some have been downright punishing to my administration politically. Back in late 1991, when I had been in office less than a year, a survey showed that a mere eighteen percent of voters thought I should be reelected. But by 1994, I was able to win reelection with sixty-two percent of the vote.

Thus the key, it seems to me, is what the Holy Father keeps stressing everywhere he goes, every time he speaks: "Be not afraid." Be bold and do the right thing. It's advice I've consistently given to the 104th Congress. If you have courage and if you are guided by sound principles, you will not only usher in an era of significant reform; you'll live to tell about it. Remember Lincoln on that parapet!

As we prepare for the twenty-first century, as we gather as Catholics in the public square, we must be ever bold. Earlier I mentioned the Holy Father's homily at Camden Yards in 1995. Permit me to conclude with the words he spoke during that homily, for they speak to the purposes of the Catholic Campaign for America:

> The Spirit God has given us is no cowardly spirit. . . . There is no evil to be faced that Christ does not face with us. There is no enemy that Christ has not already conquered. There is no cross to bear that Christ has not already borne for us, and does not now bear with us. And on the far side of every cross, we find the newness of life in the Holy Spirit. . . . This is our faith. This is our witness before the world.

God bless you and keep you.

Chapter XIV

Issues and Diversity:
A Catholic Perspective

In discussing public Catholicism, it is beneficial to try to bring some Catholic sensibility to discussions about issues related to race, ethnicity, and diversity. I think that, like a lot of people in public policy in Washington, we have lives that are in many ways very isolated. We have our public policy life in which we talk about issues. Then, we have our private, our personal, and our spiritual lives, which we often don't think about as having interconnections. I think being forced to try and bring the two together and to think about why it is we have certain policy positions and how it is our Catholic training, our Catholic background, our faith, that brings us to certain conclusions is something we don't normally think about.

A few weeks ago I was invited by a local parish, Blessed Sacrament, to be on a panel with three other people who are involved in public policy in American life, Bill Bennett, Secretary Henry Cisneros from HUD, and Chris Matthews, the *San Francisco Chronicle* bureau chief. We were asked to follow a sort of similar challenge — to think about welfare policy and social policy and how it is that we have arrived at very different perspectives on public policy based on our own understanding of our Catholic faith and our own Catholic training. I'd like to do something similar today in terms of the issue of diversity.

Although the *Catechism of the Catholic Church* does not specifically address diversity, there is a great deal in it about how the Church views the person, what personhood is, and what constitutes the relationship of the person to his/her society, to the state, and in that respect, to the whole issue of public policy. I believe it is pertinent that we address the issue of diversity, how that issue becomes a moral issue, and think about some of the challenges today with respect to issues of diversity, race, ethnicity, and civil rights.

One of the great things about the Civil Rights Movement of the 1950's and 1960's, which I think is often ignored by public commentators today, was that it was truly a grand moral revolution. It was a revolution to make the principles on which this country was founded the ideals on which we base our public policy. We have in the Declaration of Independence a statement that all men are created equal and endowed by their creator with certain inalienable rights. But for too long in the history of this nation, both before its founding and unfortunately for a significant period after its founding, that principle was not in fact enforced through the public policies of our government. For many in this society, particularly for those of African American heritage, that principle was not made a reality; and in the 1950's and 1960's, largely as a result of activity within the churches throughout the country, there was a moral struggle to make that principle public policy. It culminated in the passage of the 1964 Civil Rights Act, which took the ideal of equality of individuals and made it, in fact, the law of the land. It made it illegal for the state to consider individuals as unequal persons simply on the basis of their race, their national origin, or their sex. In fact it took that public morality and insisted that private individuals act according to that morality as well. That private individuals in their dealings with each other treat each other as individuals with equal rights and that invidious distinctions based on characteristics over which we have no control — where we were born, who our parents were, what our racial or ethnic group is — would no longer be allowed even in the private sector with respect to whom we could hire or whom we could admit to school, whom we could choose to serve in our establishments whether they be hotels, restaurants, or other public accommodations. That goal, that ideal of recognizing the worth of the individual, the worth of the person, the equality before the law of each person in this society was, I think, in many respects one of the grandest moments of our democracy. This truly made the words of the founders of this nation a reality in our lives.

What has happened to that moral revolution of the 1960's, when we took those ideals and made them law and public policy in America? A great deal has happened and unfortunately a great deal of it has diverted us away from those goals and principles.

Individual and Group Rights

For the early years after the Civil Rights Revolution, we were committed in our public policies to equality before the law without regard to race, sex, or national origin. Our public policy was directed in that way, and I think everyone believed at the time that what was being guaranteed was an equal opportunity to be able to succeed on our own efforts and on our own merit and on our own God-given talents. Individuals were the focus of this public policy. It was the individual person who was to be judged without regard to discrimination. But in the late 1960's, and exacerbated by Court decisions and by changes in the administration of Civil Rights laws in the early 1970's, we saw a transformation of these principles away from the notion of individual rights and toward the notion of group rights. Rather than simply considering individuals without respect to sex or race or national origin, our public policy tried to eliminate differences in outcomes between groups. The focus was all on group membership and not on the individual. That had a very dramatic effect not only on our public policy but on our lives. We went from saying that it should be inappropriate and improper to consider someone's racial or ethnic background or sex in determining whether he or she got a job to requiring that every person note his or her racial and ethnic affiliation to a period where now whatever you do in public life in America — whether it be applying for a job or applying to go to college, or applying for a loan at your local bank to fix up your kitchen, to practically every form you get from federal, state, or local government — you are required to state precisely those characteristics that we were

144

supposed to be moving away from as criteria for making decisions. Now, every single piece of paper that comes down from government has a little box on it where you have to check which group you belong to. What your racial background is. What your ethnic affiliation is. Your sex. Or, in the more politically correct term today, your gender.

This transformation has had, I believe, a devastating consequence for the effort to reach the very goals of the Civil Rights Movement that so unified this nation thirty years ago. Instead of promoting racial and ethnic harmony in this nation, instead of promoting a more integrated society, it has encouraged us to think of ourselves as members of groups, and it has provoked differences between those groups. It has provoked an emphasis on what makes us different from each other rather than what makes us part of one common human family.

There have been other consequences of these policies. They have not only had an impact on how we think and how we see ourselves and where we fit in this society. I believe they have had some very unintended and unfortunate consequences on the very people who were initially, at least, the intended beneficiaries of these policies. Initially, these policies were aimed at helping those who had been kept outside of society, who had been denied equal opportunity on the basis of their ancestry. The idea was to make opportunity available and to guarantee opportunity with our laws and our policies. But rather than helping those who had been on the outside, what these policies have done, in my view, is to treat individuals who are members of the targeted groups as if there are no differences between members of those groups and to treat those groups, in total, as if they are incapable of ever achieving as individuals on the basis of their own effort.

Affirmative Action

There is a lot of talk today about affirmative action policies, for example, affect White males in this society. We are told constantly by commentators on television and in our newspapers that the election in 1994 was all about White male rage; it was all about White males lashing back; it was all about those who felt that they had been harmed by some of these policies rising up in anger. Indeed, even some of those who are critics of affirmative action focus their criticism only on the impact of these policies in denying opportunity to the majority White population and to men in particular.

Not surprisingly, given my own background, my emphasis has been a little different over the years in critiquing these programs. Obviously, I am bothered that a program applies different rules to different groups and has, in effect, sometimes required a higher standard to be met by those who are White and those who are male, and that bothers me as a matter of simple justice. But it also bothers me that applying those different rules and applying those different standards sends a very invidious message to the intended beneficiaries of those policies. It says to me, it says to my children, that we can never meet the standards that are set for the majority population in this society. It says that there is something inherent about us that will not allow us to meet those standards. Rather than promoting the idea of equality, it promotes the concept of inequality — of permanent inequality. Why do I say that? I say that because when you take apart the public policies that are promoted in the name of affirmative action in the United States, you find that the standards are, in fact, very different for different groups. The way in which these programs operate in the real world is often very different than how those who support them think they operate or claim they operate. I'd like to address affirmative action in higher education, because that's the area that I'm most familiar with. We have, for example, at the University of California, a fair amount of data on how the affirmative action admissions process treats the students who apply to the system. What we know from the empirical data that was collected, mostly in the 1980's, about the admissions process particularly at Berkeley, which is the campus for which we have some of the best information, is that if you are White or Asian, in order to be admitted as a freshman on the U.C. Berkeley campus, you have to have a grade-point average of 4.0 and SAT scores that are 300 points higher than the average for students who are admitted who are Hispanic or Black. Black and Hispanic students, on average, come in with a 3.5 grade-point, one-half point lower than the figure for Whites and Asians.

Defenders of affirmative action say that this is necessary because those who benefit from this admission policy are people who have been disadvantaged in some way — they have gone to unequal school systems, they have not had the benefit of the opportunities that many Whites and Asians have had in their pre-college experience. Well, the university itself set out to find out information about the students who were admitted in the affirmative action program. In terms of earnings, the Black and Hispanic students looked pretty much like other Americans — they came from families that earned roughly $34-35,000 per year in 1989, which was the year the study was done, and in that year that income was the median income for families with four members. So they were pretty much middle Americans. The university also asked questions about the kind of educational experiences these students had had. It turned out that the overwhelming majority of the students admitted in the affirmative action program had not gone to inner-city schools. Most of them had gone to suburban school systems and most of them had gone to school systems that were majority White. They lived in integrated neighborhoods and had gone to schools that looked an awful lot like the schools of the White and Asian students, who were subjected to very different criteria. It also turned out, when the university actually took an opinion survey and spoke with a representative sample of these students, that most of the students said that they had never encountered discrimination growing up. In fact, one Mexican American girl noted that she did not even know that there had been a history of racism and discrimination against her people and that she only discovered this fact when she got to the university — and I think she was probably helped along in that process by some of her professors. The point is that this policy presumes that if your name is Chavez or if you are African American, you are going to come from a certain background and you are going to be at a certain disadvantage. Therefore, the same rules that apply to other students in the university system are not applied to you; you simply cannot meet that same standard. This is done in the name of helping, in the name of trying to include and trying to make persons a part of a community. We are saying that we are going to let you in, but under different rules.

How many people who promote such policies, if their children brought home grades that were below what was expected or SAT scores below what was expected, would accept the notion that the system was against them and that they should not have to measure up to the same rules as everyone else? I'm always fascinated. In fact, I got into a debate with the dean of the law school of The University of Texas a few years ago, after he wrote defending the differential admissions policy, particularly regarding LSAT scores at his own university. I openly challenged him to explain what would happen when his son came home with law boards at the level of the Mexican American and Black students he was admitting — what would his response be to that? Would he accept excuses from his son or would he decide that either his son was not working hard enough or that his son needed some help to bring those scores up? I never got an answer. This kind of patronizing attitude toward members of minority groups, in the long haul, will have very damaging effects on the self-esteem of those minorities, on their concept of themselves, and on their belief that they truly are equal in this society. Can you imagine if we decided that certain persons on football or basketball teams would be considered to have scored a touchdown if they fell ten or twenty yards short of the goal line, or that hitting the rim would score as a basket? When we take ourselves out of the very heavily loaded area of race and ethnicity and start thinking about the logical implications of our policies and how these would apply to our own children or to different games, as it were, I think we can see that there is something inherently wrong with the system that we've put in place.

Having said that and having defended the idea that our policies should be race-neutral and sex-neutral with respect to admission criteria or hiring or promotions or any other field — does that mean that I ignore what are, in fact, inequalities in outcomes in this society? No, it doesn't. For those of you who have not had occasion to walk around the neighborhoods in Washington, D.C., you don't have to walk very far to see the kind of inequality of outcome around us. The question is, how do we make a difference and how do we go about improving the life chances of those who do come from truly disadvantaged backgrounds? The way our federal government has done it is simply by substituting race, ethnicity, and sex as proxies for social and economic disadvantage. In fact, Senator Dole, back early in 1995, just after the Republicans took over the Congress and had some sway with the Congressional Research Service, asked the CRS to conduct a study of all federal regulations in this area of affirmative action. He came up with about 168 different regulations which, in one form or another, grant preferences on the basis of race or ethnicity, or in some instances sex, to members of groups. The fascinating thing about some of these regulations is that they talk explicitly about social and economic disadvantage. That's the criteria — you're supposed to give contracts to socially and economically disadvantaged companies. I always find this interesting in some areas, for example in the awarding of broadcast licenses by the FCC, because anyone wealthy enough to be able to get into the process of bidding for a television or radio license is hardly economically disadvantaged by any standard. But, in fact, the government doesn't just leave it at that. It doesn't just use those terms; it then defines what socially and economically disadvantaged means. It means belonging to a group that is defined by race and ethnicity. The "disadvantage" in the regulations is actually defined as being Black or being Hispanic or being a Pacific

Islander or being an Aleut or being an Eskimo or being anyone of a number of different groups. In one of the regulations having to do with the awarding of housing contracts under HUD, being a Hasidic Jew is defined as socially and economically disadvantaged. So what the government has done is to use ethnicity and race and ancestry as proxies for social and economical disadvantage. In practical consequence, the members of those groups that are given preference, who are able to take advantage of those preferences are, in fact, the most successful members of those groups.

I'm always fascinated by those who say we need affirmative action in higher education because we have such problems in unemployment, we have such high poverty rates in the Latino community or in the Black community. But they never seem to notice that those who are in poverty are usually people who have not completed their high school education and therefore could not possibly take advantage of affirmative action admissions to an elite institution. Those are not the target individuals; those are not the people who are able to take advantage of those programs.

We do need to be aware that there are poor in this society and there are those who, through no fault of their own, are born to parents — often single mothers — who live in communities where crime is rampant, who go to schools where simply making it through the day safe and alive is a real challenge, much less learning how to read or write or add or subtract. We have to understand that there are those problems in this society. But the question is, how do we deal with those problems and how do we come up with programs that will help improve the chances of individuals who are from those socially and economically disadvantaged backgrounds? And how do we know whether or not the policy that we have in place in the name of diversity or in the name of affirmative action is the right policy?

Quite clearly, if you look at the statistics alone over the last twenty-five years, you see very little change in social and economic disadvantages despite the policies that we've had in place for that period. The numbers with respect to the poor, the unemployed, and so on remain pretty much the same. We have spent quite a substantial amount — one estimate is something like four percent of our gross national product — on affirmative action programs in both the public and private sectors in the U.S., and we've not touched at all those who are truly disadvantaged in this society.

School Choice

I think the only way that we can help those who are truly disadvantaged, who do live in communities that are rife with social problems, is to focus on those communities and, in particular, to focus on the education of children. The fact is that impoverished children often attend public schools that do not provide an education. While we debate in Congress whether or not we're cutting education or simply having smaller increases in education in terms of the money that goes into public schools around the country, most of the legislators are unwilling to deal with the one solution which might, in fact, open doors to those who live in poor communities, offer the opportunity that often these very same legislators and often the people who live in the White House take advantage of themselves — the opportunity to send their children to schools of their choice.

I look back on my own background growing up as a Catholic child in Albuquerque, New Mexico, and Denver, Colorado, and the opportunity the Catholic schools provided for me. My father had a ninth-grade education; my mother had a high-school education. I did not come from a middle-class background; I came from a working-class background. My father worked as a house painter for most of my childhood and my mother worked as a waitress and as a saleswoman. She worked her way up to being an assistant buyer in a clothing store in Denver. But had it not been for the education I received in the Catholic schools in Albuquerque and Denver, I literally would not have had the opportunities that I have today.

I remember that it was a struggle sometimes for my parents to pay the tuition, but the tuition, when I went to school, was

about $100 per year. By the time I ended school it may have gotten
up to $200 per year, but that was still in the 1950's and 1960's — it
was an amount my family could afford to pay. Catholic school
education is a lot more expensive today. The idea that we deny
those who are poor the ability to make that choice — to choose
schools for their children that provide discipline and provide
training in the basics, that actually teach children a little bit about
grammar, not just have courses that make them feel good about
themselves and raise their self-esteem on the basis of feel-good
lectures — this seems to me one of the ways that we can help
those who are truly disadvantaged.

Not all parents will, in fact, choose to send their children to
parochial schools or other private schools, even if given that
opportunity, so I don't think we can ignore what goes on in the
public schools either. I think that there has to be an emphasis,
particularly by those of us who are concerned about these
problems, with the content of public education. In public
education itself, we have looked to the schools to solve all of our
social problems. There's as much time devoted to dealing with
social issues as there is to dealing with the basics of education. We
spend a lot of time teaching children about drugs, alcohol, AIDS,
sex, conflict resolution, and the environment, and very little time
teaching them the kinds of things that we learned when we went
to school.

Focusing on education and on the opportunities it provides is
terribly important. If we are talking about the truly disadvantaged,
we have to recognize that we do have to spend money on these
problems, we do have to provide for compensatory education. But
spending that money wisely is very different from simply
increasing the budget, which is what we have done for the last
thirty years. I am often amused when I talk to college audiences
who think that the effect of the Republicans on Capital Hill and the
twelve years of Republican presidency has, in fact, ruined American
public education. If it were not for this influence, they believe,
everyone would be doing very well because there would be more

and more money poured into the schools. Many of these students have no idea that before 1965 not a penny of federal dollars was ever spent on any public school in America. There was no federal aid to public schools before the Elementary and Secondary Education Act of 1965. I don't know that more money is the solution and I don't think it is right for conservatives also to say that money is not a part of the problem at all. We do have to spend money, but we have to spend it wisely. How we spend it and whether it's government money or whether it's done in the private sector, I think, is what differentiates conservatives from liberals.

Racial Tension

The whole idea of America as a nation made up of individuals is critical at this point in our history. We now look around us, and the events of the last year in particular tell us that we have become more divided on the basis of color than we have been at any time in the recent past. It is a very frightening prospect to me to look around and to see the kind of sentiments that now routinely get expressed in college newspapers around the country. I was in California and I saw a reference to an ad that had been written in one of the UC campuses' newspapers that was filled with vitriolic racial hatred. In this instance it was a Black student activist writing an anti-Semitic diatribe. It isn't just Black anti-Semitism or Black racism; there is a lot of White racism that goes on around the country too. We are, in fact, becoming more and more divided and more and more pulled apart on the basis of race and color.

A Challenge

At the very time we're becoming a more diverse country — the whole demography of the United States is changing — we have at our hands a challenge. We are becoming more ethnically diverse, and the very fact that our ancestry is different is a real challenge to us to figure out ways we can overcome those differences in our backgrounds. How can we once again forge this sense of unity, forge this sense that we are, in fact, one nation and one people made up of individuals and that those individuals have to be the focus of our respect and the focus of our attention? How can we convince ourselves that we must not divide the country up into these competing and warring factions? Real diversity means that we have to recognize our differences, and find bridges to allow us to overcome those differences and forge a sense once again of ourselves as one people.

And that, I think, is the real challenge to us as Catholics and the real challenge to us in looking at public policies that move us in that direction, or away from that direction. That ought to be our bottom line. Every time we look at solutions to problems that purport to send us in one direction, we have to question whether we are going down the road to greater equality, greater respect for the person, and greater respect for the individual, or whether we are not. The challenge to us as Catholics and as Americans is to make sure that we do go down the road to unity.

Catholic Identity: Getting the Message Out

When I was first asked to address the topic of Catholic identity, I thought it an unfortunate topic. After all, we Catholics seem to be going through an identity *crisis* these days. We no longer seem to have a clear understanding as to who we are. The media are forever playing up our divisions and differences. Studies have shown a significant drop in Mass attendance and the use of the Sacrament of Penance. There has been a woeful decline in the knowledge of the most basic facts of the faith among Catholics. We no longer seem so culturally identifiable as we did when we all abstained from meat on Friday, had our May processions in the streets around the church, and carried our missals to Mass.

But as I reflected on these facts of Catholic life, I came to see that Catholics continue to be quite culturally identifiable even if not as distinctively so as in the past.

Cultural Impact

Many years ago I was on a transcontinental flight. When it was time for the food service, I was asked by the flight attendant whether I wanted a fish or chicken meal. It was Friday, and I was reminded of the fact when the flight attendant had given me the option of a fish entree. Catholics had a profound cultural impact simply by being Catholic back then. Airlines, public schools, corporate cafeterias all acknowledged the Catholic discipline of the Friday abstinence by always making fish available on that weekly day of penance.

Back then, the message of Catholic identity was widely disseminated by Catholics simply being Catholics, with no fanfare, no banners, no television specials; in this case just the simple discipline of abstaining from meat on Friday. And for all the jokes that came to surround this Catholic practice, and for all the times it was observed in the breach, it gave honor to Jesus Christ. Non-Catholics knew we were not eating meat as a corporate act of penance to commemorate Our Lord's death on Friday. Through that act, we identified ourselves as Catholics. But far more importantly, we brought to the attention of the world, week by week by week, that Christ had died for our sins.

Last year I was on a airline flight on a Friday in Lent, a day on which a Catholic in the United States is still bound *by Church law* to abstain from flesh meat. I was offered a choice of two meals by the flight attendant, one chicken, the other beef. I asked if there was a meal without meat since it was a Friday in Lent. "Oh, no," the flight attendant reassured me, "Catholics don't have to fast on Friday any more." This individual was in error, of course, regarding the discipline of Lent, but even *she*, a non-Catholic, was aware of the fact that the Church had changed her previous discipline on the matter. She, for all her presumed indifference to Catholicism, knew something of the ebb and flow of its customs and practices.

In preparing this presentation, I began to reflect on incidents in my life recently that showed that there was indeed still a Catholic identity that had its public impact.

About two months ago, I was talking with two men in the lobby of the hotel where I was staying. Somehow the fact that my wife and I had nine children came up in the conversation. The one man asked me, "Oh, are you a fish eater?" I looked at him rather quizzically. The other interjected by way of clarification, "What he means is, 'Are you a mackerel snapper?' "

I had grown up in Pittsburgh, and I knew what that expression meant. It was a local slang expression for Catholics. "Yes," I said. "I'm a mackerel snapper."

On another occasion, my family and I were in a department store. As I held the elevator door for my wife and children to enter, a man already on the elevator watched the entire clan file in. As the doors closed, he turned to me, a perfect stranger, and asked, "What's your parish?" In the light of the evidence of all those children, he simply, and in this case justifiably, concluded that we were Catholic.

One evening I was watching the Woody Allen movie *Manhattan*. In the film Woody Allen was commenting on the sad fact that relationships seemed so transitory in the contemporary world. As he and his girlfriend walked through Central Park, he said ruefully to her: "You know, the only ones who mate for life any more are Canada geese and Catholics." I doubt Woody Allen ever sat through a Catholic theology course on marriage, but even he knew the Church's teaching on the indissolubility of matrimony.

Recently on an Amtrak train a young man sitting across from me in the dining car watched me grade papers. Finally he could contain his curiosity no longer and asked me where I taught. I told him I was a professor at the seminary for the training of priests in the Archdiocese of Philadelphia. He identified himself as a law student at the University of Pennsylvania and said he was of the Jewish faith. His parents were Orthodox Jews. Finally he said, "May I ask a question about the Catholic Church?" "Of course," I said. "What is it?" "Why," he asked, "can't priests get married?"

The Catholic Church fascinates our contemporary culture. It intrigues and frightens at the same time.

Public Witness

What is the point of so many apparently disparate anecdotes about the way Catholics are perceived? My principal point is that there IS a Catholic identity in this country and by and large it is correctly perceived.

Catholics are still perceived as entering into indissoluble marriages in which they are usually more generous than their non-Catholic peers with the gift of life. There is the accurate perception that Catholic priests embrace a sacrificial life of celibacy, and that Catholics generally are given to corporate acts of penance. These facts are usually not fully understood and certainly are not entirely appreciated by the non-Catholic American public, but they *are* known, and the facts are generally accurate. When I was referred to as a "mackerel snapper" recently, I was amazed to think that Catholics are still identified with a corporate act of mortification some *three decades* after the law mandating it in this country had been abrogated by the country's Bishops! That ought to be some indication to the Bishops of the powerful witness provided by mandated corporate acts of devotion! When I thought of the manner in which the message of Catholic identity "got out" when I was young, it was precisely through the seemingly endless acts of devotion and piety which I saw performed among Catholics. The women serving up our lunches in the public school cafeteria with the black smudges on their foreheads on Ash Wednesday. The men on the streetcar in Pittsburgh crossing themselves as they rode past St. Mary's Church. The women covering their heads before walking into a Catholic Church and the men uncovering theirs. The fingers dipped into the holy water font. The lighting of votive candles. The statue of St. Joseph in the kitchen window looking *out* of the house as a sign of his protective solicitude for the children who had left home. Even though many of these customs are gone, there are still plenty of distinguishing characteristics of the Catholic.

Defining Catholic Identity

Of course, if we want to talk about getting the message out about Catholic identity, we want to make sure that we have the identity straight. For all the charm of many cherished Catholic customs that provided Catholics with a sense of identity in the past, it is critically important to look beyond them to what it was that they had expressed. They had not been thought up by some liturgical committee and imposed on the people of God. More often than not, they were natural, spontaneous expressions of faith and love which became sanctified through generations of use and which sometimes became legally sanctioned.

First and last, a Catholic's identity is found in his relationship with Jesus Christ. If that is lacking, quaint Catholic customs, and even great acts of Catholic charity and service, are worthless. All that a Catholic does, from his religious practices to his professional work, is to be imbued with the Spirit of Christ. As Paul of Tarsus, the itinerant Pharisee and tentmaker, said: "It is no longer I who live but Christ who lives in me!" And Christ was living and working in Paul just as much when he was measuring out the fabric and stitching it up into a tent as when he was preaching and writing his epistles. If Christ is not living in us, then there is no Catholic identity and no message to get out.

The truly distinguishing traits of Catholic identity, and there are indeed many, all refer to Jesus Christ: Baptism, in which we are joined to Christ; the Mass, in which we plead His sacrifice; Penance, in which we receive His forgiveness; our love for His Blessed Mother; our veneration of His closest friends, the saints; the Rosary, in which we meditate on His life; pilgrimages; votive candles; men and women in religious habits; chant and incense. These are all marks of the Catholic's identity, and they are all ways in which the Catholic relates to Christ and brings others to Him.

True Catholics

But how does the message of this identity get out? There is in The Catholic Campaign for America the legitimate desire to bring articulate Catholic spokesmen and women into the public forum. Also, there are Catholic individuals or groups who will sometimes raise tens of thousands of dollars to take out full-page advertisements in the elite newspapers of the United States to bypass the bias of so many in the media. To get our message out, books must be published, press conferences held, rallies organized. But it must be said very forthrightly that those efforts have true efficacy *only* if the individuals involved are constantly undergoing interior conversion, if they are striving to live lives of total fidelity to Christ and His Church, and if they have a love for neighbor which is palpable.

The massive struggle between good and evil in which we are now engaged is no place for superficial Catholics who love the beauty of their ethnic customs but malign the Pope or openly dissent from Church teaching or discipline. In the Pope's recent encyclical, *Evangelium Vitae*, he has spoken of this struggle in truly apocalyptic terms. Our Holy Father sees a Culture of Death locked in mortal combat with a civilization of love. This is no place or time for the fainthearted. The Pope sees civilization itself faced with the danger of its own self-destruction. As the Holy Father said, not only in *Evangelium Vitae* (No. 59) but also in his *Letter to Families* (Nov. 21, 1994): "We are facing an immense threat to life: not only to the life of individuals but also to that of civilization itself."

The goal of The Catholic Campaign for America is nothing other than the transformation of culture according to the mind of Christ. But such transformation will ultimately be wrought by individuals not by organizations, no matter how good they are. The most effective way in which Catholics can get the message out about Catholic identity is for them to be entirely faithful Catholics. There is absolutely no substitute for this.

I did not grow up a Catholic. And it was not "professional Catholics" who brought me into the Church. For example, as necessary as the media ministry of a Bishop Fulton Sheen was, and as many souls as it helped save, it did not touch me in the least. I was vaguely aware of him as a television personality. I now listen to and relish his tapes, and I read his books, and I share them with non-Catholics. But what worked its magic on me was not that photogenic, eloquent, and holy priest. It was Mae Brenckle, our next-door neighbor, among others.

Every morning at 6:15 I would hear the car engine start up in the neighbor's driveway beside our home. Spring, summer, fall, winter. The car engine would start up 6:15 in the summer when the sun was already beginning to warm the pasture behind our home and the birds were welcoming the dawn. It started up at 6:15 on the cold, dark mornings of winter after the snow had been shoveled out of the drive and the ice scraped from the windows. I could hear the car start up between the crashes of thunder during an early morning storm in the spring. Morning after morning after morning. During the school year, during summer vacation, when my alarm went off and when it didn't, I could count on the sound of Mae Brenckle's car starting up. Finally one day I asked my mother if Mrs. Brenckle had to leave so early to get to work. The answer astounded me. "No," my mother said. "She doesn't have to be at work until later. She's a Catholic. She goes to Mass every morning before work."

I remember being totally amazed when I heard that. Such fidelity, such regularity, such dependability. And it was not because her employment required that she get up so early every morning and endure often inclement weather. It was love. It was love for her Lord in the Eucharist whom she went to receive day after day.

In a way, the Catholicism of Mae Brenckle was a public Catholicism. She gave public witness to her faith day after day in her attendance at Holy Mass. It is that kind of Catholicism which will eventually transform society. There can be absolutely no substitute for the one-on-one witness of Catholics to their neighbors, relatives, and co-workers.

In his *Apostolic Exhortation on the Family*, the Holy Father declares: "Family, become what you are!" He also declares to the laity: "Catholic laity, become what you are!" Simply by being fully Catholic, we will get the message out. Simply by being fully Catholic, we begin to effect the transformation of society.

The Source of Catholic Life

The Pope is not a layman, of course. But he does teach us what it is to be a Christian in the world. During his last visit to the United States, the Holy Father, through his actions, commended certain practices to the lay faithful of the United States which will strengthen our identity and have a profound effect on getting our message out.

First of all, of course, the Pope demonstrated to all the world that the center, source, and summit of Catholic life is the Eucharist. Every day he celebrated Mass with tens upon tens of thousands. He showed that nothing except sin can separate the Catholic from the love of God as it is offered to Him in the Mass. Through his demeanor of reverence and recollection he showed the love and respect which Catholics have for the Mass. There is no way in which the identity of the Catholic could ever be separated from the Mass, from the sacrifice of Christ on Calvary. Not only in terms of the general cultural perceptions of what it means to be a Catholic, but profoundly in terms of the Pope's own witness, the Mass and Catholic identity are surely indelibly etched in the minds of the American public. Any message which we are to get out with regard to the identity of Catholics must include the centrality of the Mass, that act which actually brings the Church about, that act that constitutes Catholics as the Body of Christ, which they consume at the eucharistic celebration.

Public Prayer

During the Pope's visit it was interesting to note the private devotions which, through his quiet, steady example, he commended to the Catholics of America. The Pope scheduled a visit to St. Patrick's Cathedral in New York City, which was filled to capacity as thousands waited on the streets outside. The reason for stopping in the Cathedral was to lead the faithful in what is basically a private devotion, the recitation of the Rosary. Here is surely one of the most distinguishing marks of Catholic identity, the string of beads with the crucified Christ.

How do we get out the message of the importance of mental prayer in general and of the Rosary in particular? Fundamentally by praying. I often wonder at the quiet, yet profound way in which the message of the importance of prayer could be disseminated by Catholic men once again unabashedly praying the Rosary in the course of the many nonproductive interstices that make up any day: the ride on the train or subway, the drive to work, the walk to the office.

When the Pope visited Baltimore there was much excitement about the fact that he was going to visit the beautifully restored neoclassical basilica of St. Mary's, the first cathedral in the United States. News releases indicated that the church's bells would ring again, for the first time in over twenty years. Yet when the Pope entered the basilica, it became immediately apparent why a stop was scheduled there. It was not simply to admire the architecture, as admirable as it was. As soon as he entered the church, the Holy Father went right to the prie-dieu before the tabernacle, where he went down on his knees in prayer before Our Lord in the Blessed Sacrament. In that gesture, he commended to the faithful, regular visits to the Blessed Sacrament in order to deepen their relationship with Our Lord. Worship of Our Lord in the Blessed Sacrament is another distinctive mark of Catholic identity.

I used to work for the National Bank of Mexico. On one occasion I was walking through the colonial part of Mexico City near the *zócalo* (public square) talking to a Mexican banker, who almost in the middle of a sentence disappeared through a dark door leading off the narrow street. I followed him a bit confused. When my eyes adjusted to the darkness, I realized we were in a church. I saw the banker on his knees, and then I noticed the Blessed Sacrament in the monstrance on the altar. The banker remained on his knees for two, maybe three minutes, at which point he got up, genuflected, went through the small door back out onto the street where he picked up on the conversation about Mexico's external debt without uttering a word about his little detour. It is through truly countless little acts of piety and devotion, it is through an offering up of one's professional work to God, that the Catholic message will find its way into the fabric of our society with all its transforming power.

The Disintegration of the State

There is a final point that I would like to draw from the Pope's last visit to the United States. I believe it is critically important for those of us involved in the public presentation of the Church's message. There are unspeakable horrors being perpetrated in our society that not only threaten the common good but which are at this very moment contributing mightily to our social disintegration. We are all familiar with the quip that if God does not punish New York and Washington, He owes Sodom and Gomorrah an apology. We must forcefully condemn these evils, not only as Catholics but as American citizens. However, at the same time, we have to be cautious that we do not become shrill in our righteous indignation.

There are those who listened closely to our Holy Father who were disappointed that he seemed to be softening his message. It did not seem as harsh and as challenging as on other visits. There is some truth to that in my opinion, but it would appear to be part of the Holy Father's overall plan in fulfilling his role in the transformation of contemporary culture, a strategy which we might well consider in our Catholic Campaign for America.

The Pope had already delivered his searing critique and thunderous denunciation of the murderous evils of the Culture of Death in *Evangelium Vitae*. And there are few societies on earth more deserving of that appellation than the United States of America. He spoke there of "atrocious crimes" and "murderous violence." He said that those who would choose abortion have an attitude that "is shameful and utterly reprehensible." He said that the encyclical dealt with "questions of extraordinary seriousness" because "crimes have assumed the nature of rights." He was here clearly thinking of countries such as the United States. And because "crimes have assumed the nature of rights," nations that had been considered civilized are reverting "to a state of barbarism." In that encyclical the Pope spoke with uncompromising severity: Whenever we see legally sanctioned abortions we are dealing with a "tyrant state," which through

immoral legislation exhibits a "tragic caricature of legality."
Indeed, the Pope warns that in a country that permits and
promotes abortion "the disintegration of the state has begun."

The Pope has been harsh in his denunciations of the evils of
our society. But the Pope is aware of the full nature of man. He is
aware of the fact that the human reality is described by the
doctrine of the *imago dei* as well as the doctrine of original sin.
Man truly has the capacity for good as well as his dismaying
inclination toward evil. The Pope likes using the figure of lights
and shadows. He had already exposed the shadows in our national
life in *Evangelium Vitae.* During his last visit to the United States,
I believe he purposefully accentuated the light.

A Beacon of Hope

Time after time he called us Americans to our highest and
truest nature. He appealed not only to our altruism but to our
history. He pointed out that the United States had always stood as a
beacon of hope to the world, as an example of charity and goodness
and inclusiveness. He said:

> For nations and peoples emerging from a long period of trial,
> your country stands upon the world scene as a model of a
> democratic society at an advanced stage of development. Your
> power of example carries with it heavy responsibilities. Use it
> well, America! Be an example of justice and civic virtue,
> freedom fulfilled in goodness, at home and abroad!

The Pope's remarks were reminiscent of the great pro-life
Democratic Governor of Pennsylvania, Robert Casey, who, as we
know, was prevented by the forces of Bill Clinton from addressing
the last National Democratic Convention. In 1994 Governor Casey
addressed the gathering of The Catholic Campaign for America.
When he reached the topic of abortion in his prepared remarks, he
stopped and departed from his text. He set his jaw and clenched his
teeth and declared that abortion was simply un-American. This
lifetime politician and public servant, this American of Americans,

could think of no more condemnatory way of characterizing abortion than by repeating over and over: It is simply un-American; abortion is un-American!

When the Pope was celebrating Mass in the pouring rain in Giants Stadium, he articulated universal truths which had been affirmed in the very founding of this nation. "The right to life," the Pope said, "is the first of all rights. It is the foundation of democratic liberties and the keystone of the edifice of civil society. Both as Americans and as followers of Christ, American Catholics must be committed to the defense of life in all its stages and in every condition."

The softer tone and the more encouraging words were a purposeful tactic, I believe, adopted by this Pope for his visit to the United States. He is not interested in "scoring points," in climbing up in the popularity polls, in being reelected. He has no goal or objective other than the transformation of our society according to the mind of Christ. This means a society in which we realize that our greatest joy and happiness comes in service to others, especially those who are weakest and most vulnerable. The Pope has many times clearly articulated the dangers and the dark shadows in our national life. During this visit, it seemed His Holiness wanted to appeal to all that is good and wholesome and generous and noble in our national life.

He said, "I come as one who has an abiding hope in America's noble destiny."

Fear

But this genius of a man, this psychologist, this student of the human psyche *par excellence*, realizes that what keeps us Americans from being good and wholesome and generous and noble is not mean-spiritedness and hatred and pettiness; it is fear — mind-numbing, gut-wrenching fear.

I have watched this man and read his works and followed his steps from the time he ascended to the Chair of Peter. I remember vividly his words at the first Mass he celebrated as Supreme Pontiff. He addressed the world, all nations, all cultures, all peoples, and told them not to fear Christ. He told them to throw open their doors to Christ and invite Him in. Christ, he said, posed no threat to any of them.

I have heard that theme many times over the last seventeen years. But even though it was familiar to me, I was not prepared for the urgency with which the Pope returned to it during this last visit. We know that he believes that the world is faced with a crisis of the greatest magnitude. His sense of urgency is palpable. And never did it seem to come across with greater insistence than in this last visit. And we ought to see his words directed with particular keenness to The Catholic Campaign for America.

With a profound sense of history, the Pope called Catholics to respond to the call of the third millennium of Christianity, and his theme was courage, not fear. His last day in this country, he reminded us: "The challenge of the great jubilee of the year 2000 is the new evangelization: a deepening of faith and a vigorous response to the Christian vocation to holiness and service. This is what the successor of Peter has come to Baltimore to urge upon each one of you: the *courage* to bear witness to the Gospel of our Redemption."

Speaking before the United Nations, the Pope acknowledged that, despite the demise of the Cold War and a diminished risk of nuclear destruction, for the nations of the world "fear for the future and of the future remains."

He continued:

> In order to ensure that the new millennium now approaching
> will witness a new flourishing of the human spirit, mediated
> through an authentic culture of freedom, men and women must
> learn to conquer fear. We must learn not to be afraid, we must
> rediscover a spirit of hope and a spirit of trust.

In Giants Stadium the Pope told his congregation that it was fear which crippled them and kept them from being what they could be.

And in Central Park the theme of "Do not be afraid!" was particularly strong. After the conclusion of the Mass, he spoke informally to the assembled thousands and finished his remarks with words of encouragement: "Don't be afraid. Have courage. Have no fear. Don't be afraid. Don't be afraid!" And I thought to myself, "Wait a minute. Why does he keep insisting on our not being afraid? He's speaking to Americans. We are the strongest, the mightiest nation on earth! What do we have to be afraid of?"

Then I gradually realized how gripped with fear we in America actually are. We are so terrified of little unborn babies and the demands they bring with them, that we slaughter 1.5 million of them a year. We try frantically to export that fear to developing nations through governmental agencies and many of our largest and most powerful private foundations. Through our foreign aid we try to hold poorer countries hostage to that same fear.

We fear the old, frail, comatose patient lying in bed with feeding tubes running into his arms. We fear him and want to yank the tubes, pull the plug. And if he doesn't die soon enough, we want to kill him.

We fear the demands of married life and parenthood, and so we flee from spouse and children.

We fear that there might be some sensual pleasure that we might miss, and so we indulge ourselves in pornography. There are those who would run the risk of killing themselves rather than endure the thought that there was some sensual delight left unsavored.

We are crippled by fear and driven by fear at the same time. We do not trust Christ, and so we do not heed His words. He said that if we wanted to find ourselves and know true joy we must deny ourselves, take up our cross, live for others. But we are afraid to. Jesus said that if we would find life, we must die to self. But instead, out of fear, we cling selfishly to ourselves. As the Dominican theologian Augustine DiNoia puts it: "We have to realize that dying to self is not fatal." Fear is America's greatest problem.

Scripture tells us how to deal with fear. The Apostle who was Our Lord's most beloved writes: "There is no fear in love; but perfect love casts out fear" (1 Jn 4:18).

Do Not Be Afraid

During the Mass in Central Park, the Pope tried ever so earnestly to dispel the fears of the American people:

The Gospel tells us not only that Mary was surprised and confused by the words of the angel, but that she was afraid. Yes, Mary was afraid, just as we are often afraid! And the angel said, "Do not fear, Mary. For you have found favor with God" (Lk 1:30). Like Mary, you must not be afraid to allow the Holy Spirit to help you become intimate friends of Christ. Like Mary, you must put aside any fear, in order to take Christ to the world in whatever you do — in marriage, as single people in the world, as students, as workers, as professional people. Christ wants to go to many places in the world, and to enter many hearts, through you.

The Holy Father then continued his meditations on the joyous mysteries of the Rosary by reflecting on the Nativity, and touched again on the theme of fear:

[I]n the third joyful mystery of the rosary, the birth of the Son of God, (is) announced by angels to the shepherds. "You have nothing to fear. . . . This day in David's city a savior has been born to you. . . . In a manger you will find an infant wrapped in swaddling clothes." St. Luke tells us that the shepherds said to one another: "Let us go over and see this child." And they went and found the child with Mary and Joseph. That is what we too must do! We must go to this child, this man, the Son of God, at whatever inconvenience, at whatever risk to ourselves, because to know and love him will truly change our lives.

At this point, the Pope became intensely personal:

I remember a song I used to sing in Poland as a young man, a song which I still sing as pope, which tells about the birth of the Savior. On Christmas night, in every church and chapel, this

song would ring out, repeating in a musical way the story told in
the Gospel. It says: "In the silence of the night, a voice is heard:
'Get up, shepherds, God is born for you! Hurry to Bethlehem to
meet the Lord.' "

And then the Pope did a startling thing in order to dispel the
fears of the American people.

What was it the Pope did? What did this diplomat who helped
turn the course of history, who helped pulverize the foundations of
Marxist tyranny in Eastern Europe, actually do? What did this poet,
author, academician with two earned doctorates, this linguist,
playwright, head of state; what did this Bishop of Rome, High
Priest of the Universal Church, Patriarch of the West, Primate of
Italy, Archbishop and Metropolitan of the Roman Province and
Sovereign of the Vatican City State do? It was something quite
remarkable. Before the 130,000 gathered in Central Park and the
millions who watched him from around the world, he became as a
little child.

This giant of our millennium sat there and, in the presence of
millions, without a trace of self-consciousness, began to sing the
simple, melodious refrain of a child's Christmas carol. And in that
tender, vulnerable moment his critics were unexpectedly disarmed,
his enemies were struck speechless, his detractors silenced — and
his admirers were moved to tears with memories of childhood
innocence and simple family joys. For that moment, the hand of
the abortionist was stayed at the sight of the innocent Child in
swaddling clothes.

"America," he seemed to say, "you have nothing to fear from
innocence or purity or justice or goodness."

And in that graced moment the 130,000 gathered in Central
Park themselves became as little children. Right there in the
middle of the city that never sleeps, right there in the middle of
relentless, fast-paced, jaded New York, those in the presence of the
Holy Father were blessed by God with the gift of spiritual
childhood. At the conclusion of the Pope's homily they all at one
moment — because they were all moved by the One Spirit —

began to sing sweetly and softly the familiar lines of "Silent Night."
In that moment of gentleness and peace the gathered
Catholics presented their Holy and Beloved Father with an early
Christmas present. And they offered it to their nation as well. They
seemed to say to all America, "Please, you have nothing to fear
from us and our teachings. The message of the Catholic Church is
no more to be feared than a Christmas lullaby. In it you will find
peace and hope and joy. In imitation of our Holy Father, who is the
Vicar of Christ, the Servant of the Servants of God, we want to
show you by our lives and our words that it is love, and love alone,
that casts out fear."

CATHOLICS IN THE PUBLIC SQUARE

From Our Sunday Visitor

The Role of Catholics in American Life, Culture, and Politics

What role should Catholics take in today's complex society? How much should Faith affect politics? This ground-breaking new work, edited by former U.S. Ambassador to the Vatican Thomas Patrick Melady, takes a critical look at the role of Catholics in contemporary society through topics such as the importance of the lay voice, the integration of Faith in a corporate environment, and the application of the Church's teachings to life and work.

Explore what it means to be a Catholic voice crying out in a secular wilderness with such notable contributors as Mary Cunningham Agee, Robert P. Casey, Henry J. Hyde, Thomas S. Monaghan, Michael Novak, and Father Richard John Neuhaus.

About the Editor

Thomas Patrick Melady served as the U.S. Ambassador to the Holy See from 1989-1993. He is the author of Our Sunday Visitor's **The Ambassador's Story: The United States and the Vatican in World Affairs.**

Catholics in the Public Square: The Role of Catholics in American Life, Culture, and Politics

Edited by Thomas Patrick Melady

No. 0-87973-**752**-2, hardcover, $17.95, 160 pp.

Available at bookstores. MasterCard, VISA, and Discover customers can order direct from

Our Sunday Visitor by calling **1-800-348-2440**.

Or send payment plus $3.95 shipping/handling to:

 OUR SUNDAY VISITOR
200 Noll Plaza • Huntington, IN 46750

Your Source for Outstanding Catholic Materials